gcs

J. Enoch Powell

Joseph Chamberlain

with 109 illustrations

THAMES AND HUDSON

Frontispiece: as Colonial
Secretary; a formal portrait
by Sargent, 1896

Picture research: Georgina Bruckner MA

Filmset and printed in Great Britain by
BAS Printers Limited, Over Wallop, Hampshire

Contents

Foreword

This is a biographical study rather than a biography. The one and only serious biography of Chamberlain, the six volumes of Garvin and Amery, will hold the field for many years yet.* It is impossible to work with it as a basic source, as I have done, without forming a great respect for the literary and technical power of J. L. Garvin's handling of the years to 1901. Despite stylistic mannerism and the now dated perspective of the years around 1930, he built Chamberlain's life firmly into the context of the last generation of Victoria's reign. Julian Amery followed with the improbable feat of converting the materials which Garvin left behind into a convincing history of the rise of tariff reform.

The centre of gravity of the Garvin-Amery biography was heavily weighted towards the later years of Chamberlain's active life. Half their 3,700 pages are devoted to the five years 1901–06 alone. In this study I have deliberately shifted the point of balance by placing in the centre the pivotal year 1886, recently the subject of Cooke and Vincent's monograph,** with the result that the whole perspective of Chamberlain's life is altered. It is as if the years before 1886 were the unconscious preparation of that climax, and those which followed it the working out of its logical consequences.

Into a framework derived, inevitably, from Garvin-Amery, I have built material from that chronically underused source of political history, the columns of *Hansard*, and from the studies, partly acknowledged in the footnotes, of P. Fraser, D. A. Hamer and M. C. Hurst. I am grateful to Mr Mark Damazer of Gonville and Caius College, Cambridge, for reading the manuscript and making a number of acute observations from which I have profited.

House of Commons   J. ENOCH POWELL
March 1977

---

* Denis Judd, *Radical Joe* (May 1977) was published when the present book was already in proof.
** A. B. Cooke and J. Vincent, *The Governing Passion* (1974).

Introduction

When the Liberal Cabinet met on 26 March 1886, Gladstone, the Prime Minister, indicated that he intended to lay before the House of Commons a resolution proposing to establish a legislature in Dublin with power over strictly Irish affairs.

There immediately leaned forward the President of the Local Government Board, one Joseph Chamberlain, who had been returned at the general election of the previous autumn for the constituency of West Birmingham, one of seven constituencies into which the city was newly divided and all of which were won by Liberal candidates – 'we are seven', as the saying went.

He put four questions across the table to the Prime Minister:

1. Was Irish representation at Westminster to cease?
2. Was the power of taxation, including customs and excise, to be given to the Irish legislature?
3. Was the appointment of judges and magistrates to vest in the Irish authority?
4. Was the Irish legislature to have authority in every matter not specifically excluded by the Act constituting it or only in matters specifically delegated to it by statute?

Gladstone, for once, did not refine or prevaricate. He answered 'Yes' to every one of the questions. 'Then', said Chamberlain, 'I resign', whereupon he left the Cabinet room at once, accompanied by Trevelyan, the Secretary of State for Scotland.

As the door closed behind him, he turned his back upon all that his political life had been for twenty years, over ten of them in parliament. His face, and he knew it, was towards his political opponents, opponents whom he had denounced and detested, but whom he could not now help but place and maintain in power. It was the watershed of his life. Henceforward its currents would all flow in the opposite direction and find their way to an ocean undreamed of.

At the watershed of his life; a photograph taken about 1886

8

It was more than the watershed in one man's career. It was a great geological rift in the pattern of British politics. Its sequels can be traced, without any resort to fantasy, for a full two generations – until the eve at least of the Second World War.

What was it that could make such a break not merely possible but, when it came, unavoidable? What is the reconciliation, mental and emotional, between the Chamberlain before and the Chamberlain after? And what was the secret correspondence between the depths that were opened up in the 'middle walk' of this politician's life and in the new course into which the politics of Victorian Britain turned from that moment?

In real life there are no thunderclaps out of skies where not a cloud is to be discerned. The break in the Cabinet room on 26 March 1886 had been foreseeable for a few weeks, and the immediate causes which led to it can be traced back a few months further – to the earliest intimations in the summer of 1885 that Gladstone's mind was fastening upon the settlement of the Irish question as the providentially predestinated crown of his career. But though the cloud no bigger than a man's hand can be discovered some six months before by careful – and retrospective – scanning of the horizon, the speed with which the storm itself rose up the sky is still astonishing.

'The pacification of Ireland at this moment depends, I believe, on the concession to Ireland of the right to govern itself in the matter of its purely domestic business. . . . The time has come to reform altogether the absurd and irritating anachronism known as Dublin Castle. That is the work to which the new parliament will be called.' Those words, spoken at a public meeting in London in June 1885, are not Gladstone's. The speaker was Chamberlain. So close, and yet such worlds apart, were 'the right to govern itself in the matter of its purely domestic business', which Chamberlain defined in June 1885 as an essential concession, and the proposal 'to establish a legislature in Dublin with power over strictly Irish affairs', which in March 1886 blew the Liberal government and the Liberal Party to smithereens and shifted the track of events for ever.

To understand why that almost verbal variation was in reality a yawning gulf, and how that yawning gulf was crossed by Gladstone, albeit with the eventual loss and destruction of the old Liberal Party, while Chamberlain – of all people – not only halted on the brink but marched away resolutely and with growing enthusiasm in the opposite direction, it is necessary to follow Chamberlain from his entry into politics to his first encounter with the government of Ireland under the Act of Union, and then more closely to observe the impact which that encounter made upon his mind when, as a member of Gladstone's Cabinet from 1880 to 1885, he came face to face not with the municipal politics of class but with the elemental politics of nationhood and power. Under the influence of that experience the aspects of his character and thought which were no more than hinted at in his earlier career became the elements which dominated his later life.

CHAPTER I

Into Politics

In view of the coming general election the local Liberal Election Committee held a public dinner one June evening in 1868 at the Plough and Harrow Hotel, which still stands on the Hagley Road in the Edgbaston division of Birmingham. The chairman was Mr Joseph Chamberlain, aged almost thirty-two and a widower of five years' standing, who managed the patent screw partnership of Nettlefold and Chamberlain (Joseph's father). He was by birth and descent a Londoner, by religion a Unitarian, and he 'taught Sunday school' at the Church of the Messiah half a mile away down Broad Street.

Unitarianism is a form of dissent peculiarly elusive to definition, beyond the basic rejection – common to all forms of Unitarianism – of the doctrine of the Holy Trinity and the co-equal godhead of Christ; but a recent description[1] is much to the purpose: 'the Unitarian concept of humanism is agnostic about God and emphasizes the human condition and scientific progress. Unitarians have been especially responsive to the spirit of the age in which they live and have been leaders and transmitters of current thought.' In the city of Priestley and of Bolton and Watt, represented in parliament by John Bright since 1857, Mr Joseph Chamberlain, Unitarian, Liberal, philanthropic screw-maker, might rank as typical.

He was already being drawn for the first time into political activity through the Education Society, formed to promote public education at the moment of Lowe's famous dictum 'educate our masters' on the morrow of the Second Reform Act; and no sooner was the election won in November 1868, and Gladstone's government securely installed, than two things happened to Chamberlain. He became vice-chairman of the National Education League, which proposed to do for free, universal, non-sectarian, compulsory education what the Anti-Corn Law League was credited with having done for free trade a generation earlier. And he was elected a Birmingham city councillor.

The offices and works of Messrs Nettlefold and Chamberlain in Birmingham and the additional factory at Smethwick in 1871

BASKERVILLE PLACE & BROAD STREET, BIRMINGHAM.

THE PATENT SCREW WORKS, SMETHWICK.

13

Salesmanship: language, presentation and packaging to suit all customers and nationalities. The French were offered 'French heads' and their traditional 'blue paper'. *Opposite:* teaching Sunday school and managing the firm – a Birmingham photograph of the 1860s. *Below:* the patent pointed screw bore its own hole

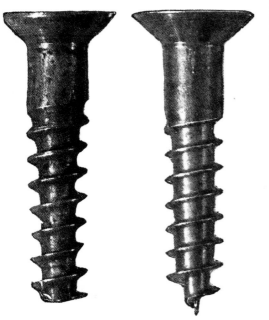

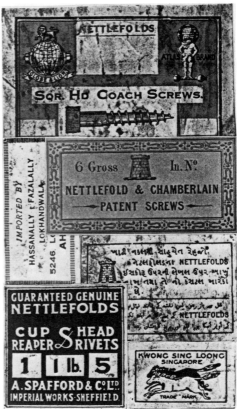

It was known that the Liberal government, having disposed of the disestablishment of the Church of Ireland in the 1869 session, was preparing a great measure on education for the session of 1870. With or without justification, the Education League, and indeed the whole of Nonconformity, took it for granted that the measure would be in line with their objectives. They were dumbfounded when in March 1870 the Education Minister, W. E. Forster, himself a Nonconformist and ex-Quaker, unveiled a Bill which fulfilled none of the League's principles but instead brought in the state and the ratepayer only to supplement the work of the churches, which were given a year's grace to occupy as much educational territory as they could.

Chamberlain stepped into the leadership of the instantaneous nationwide repudiation of the Bill, and within a fortnight was the spokesman of a confrontation between Gladstone himself and the representatives of every section of Nonconformity and many sections of Liberalism. The deputation was introduced by George Dixon MP, ex-Mayor of Birmingham, and supported by a young MP by the name of Charles Dilke. In the event the government stood by the Bill in virtually its original form; but the result was that the Liberal Party in the House of Commons was hopelessly split, over two-thirds of its members either abstaining or voting against Gladstone. The Bill was carried, but only by means of the Conservative Opposition.

A powerful prime minister, administration and party had been baulked by the stubborn assertion of a principle by an element of their own supporters. On Chamberlain, swept to the forefront of a national agitation almost at the outset of his political life, the impression must have been indelible. The spectacle was a paradigm of the very drama in which he was to play twice more, at the two climaxes of his career. The next time, too, though his role would then be the principal one, the antagonist and tragic hero would again be Gladstone. The statesman and the novice might almost have been rehearsing their parts for fifteen years ahead. Perhaps as the drama of politics revolves through its recurrent cycles, men recognize by a kind of instinct the scenes in which their own characters have cast them to play the lead.

There is something eerie in a sentence which Chamberlain wrote to George Dixon as he watched the Bill being forced through its concluding stages:

It [the Bill] is a trick to pave the way for the *one* concession to Ireland which no English parliament ought to make and which,

Sir Charles Dilke MP introduces the Education League deputation to the Prime Minister, 1870

when made, will only prepare for that repeal of the Union which I expect must come sooner or later.[2]

Did he somehow, this Birmingham Unitarian councillor, wrapped up in free compulsory non-sectarian education, have the heart of the matter in him all the time? What is certain is that in 1870, if not before, Chamberlain must already have thought out his position on Ireland and Home Rule, that it was a unionist position, and that he must have seen the question as overriding and absorbing those domestic questions with which he was publicly identified. It may be that as far back as 1868, when after the Fenian outrages of 1867 Gladstone declared himself for the disestablishment of the Church of Ireland (16 March), thus making this and the other two Irish matters of land and university, which he linked with it, issues at the election of 1868, Chamberlain had looked ahead further still and arrived silently at his own position.

During the whole remaining period of Gladstone's ministry, to the precipitate dissolution of March 1874, Chamberlain was the driving force of the National Education League in its overt denunciation of a Liberal government which steadily refused to amend the Education Act and remove the aspects that made it uncompromisingly 'dualist' as between the churches and the state as educational agencies. The League declared itself indifferent whether 'a Tory government sits on the Cabinet bench or a Liberal government passing Tory measures',[3] and it did not hesitate in its campaign to attempt to bring about at by-elections the defeat of Liberal candidates who refused to pledge themselves to support its demands.

There were times when Chamberlain himself went still further and, once again sounding a *Leitmotiv* of actions far in the future, announced that this difference of principle with Gladstone's government was one of those which justify a government's own creators and supporters in destroying it. It was, as he said in a striking article in John Morley's *Fortnightly Review* in September 1873, quoting J. S. Mill, one of those convictions in which the strength of a man's belief 'forbids him to make them the subject of compromise'.

An important by-product of all this activity was that it entailed upon Chamberlain the discipline and practice of the frequent addressing of large public meetings, and thus ripened and confirmed a style of eloquence, doubtless already his own, which was not perceptibly to vary thereafter.

At this stage in his career, without ministerial or collective constraints, he was able to speak free from the necessity of a prepared written text; and the full-scale reporting of the press of that day – and long after – fixed and held his unscripted deliverances in the files of the national and local newspapers as effectively as *Hansard*. His English was clear and vigorous, his periods uncomplicated. He practised to perfection a form of ironically humorous invective which left behind memorable phrases that would become polemics in their own right and would still be passed on with pride and relish from fathers to sons in Birmingham fifty years later. By being enveloped in a Nonconformist intensity and earnestness the Chamberlain vein of humour was saved from degenerating, even when aimed at individuals, into the 'flouts and gibes' of which Disraeli once accused Lord Salisbury of being a 'master'.

The characteristic weakness perceptible then and always in Chamberlain's eloquence was his insensitivity to sudden descent into weak endings, often marked by conventional phrases or even bathos: 'if a priest-ridden nation is very much to be pitied, a publican-ridden nation is very much to be despised' (Birmingham, 1871); 'nobody can say that the alphabet is a sectarian formulary: I have never heard that geography leads to atheism; and I have yet to be told that arithmetic is notorious heresy' (Newcastle, 1872); 'we should be the meanest and weakest of mortals if we did not pick up the gauntlet' (*Spectator*, 1873).

The years of the Education League schooled Chamberlain in another subject – electoral organization – for which he, and Birmingham, were to become famous and which, through the studies later made of it, notably by Ostrogorski,[4] was to become one of the progenitors of the modern science, or pseudo-science, of psephology. Under the Education Act of 1870, the members of the local school boards were elected by the cumulative vote, as it was then called, or proportional representation. In Birmingham the Liberals made the elementary mistake, under that system, of running too many candidates: in fact, they ran one for each of the fifteen seats, and in consequence gained only six. The next time, in 1873, the Liberals fielded only eight and returned them all, by the same 'vote as you're told' technique which had enabled them at the 1868 general election to return three members for a three-member constituency where each elector had only two votes. At that election their supporters in each ward were drilled to use their votes so as to spread the overall majority over three candidates and prevent it from being wasted on two. For such methods to work, it was necessary to identify supporters and maintain communication and discipline. In the relatively large household-franchise electorate this was the germ of the celebrated 'caucus' organization, which was supposed to have been the technical secret of the electoral hold that Chamberlain had on Birmingham for the rest of his life, and to have been the means of enabling him to cross intact with his Liberal colleagues the perilous divide when he came to it in later years. More scientific study of electoral behaviour has tended to suggest that the fame of such organizational methods greatly exceeds the reality and that the effects are not merely very limited but occur, if at all, only as an accompaniment to much deeper and subtler influences upon the pattern of voting. However, the myth, whether Chamberlain believed it or not, became part of the popular picture of him, together with his Birmingham home at Highbury and his invariable orchid buttonhole.

Certainly he fought his first parliamentary battle with no such advantage. By the time of the snap election of 1874 it happened – as it does to some politicians – that he found himself for some reason a habitually popular visiting speaker in a town with which

THE PARLIAMENTARY TRAIN.

PASSENGERS FOR WESTMINSTER.		PASSENGERS FOR COVENTRY.	
MUNTZ	Ticket 22,969		
BRIGHT	" 22,079	BURNABY	Ticket 15,735
CHAMBERLAIN	" 19,544	CALTHORPE	" 14,308

How to win three seats in a two-member constituency: the
Liberal drill song for the 1880 election, and Francis
Schnadhorst (also seen below driving the train which takes
the winners to parliament), the organizer of the Birmingham
Liberal Association and later of the National Federation

he had no personal connections, Sheffield. So he felt obliged, when the dissolution came, to allow himself to be 'drafted' as radical challenger to two Liberals in the two-member seat. He lost, and was thereby for ever reserved for Birmingham.

It was at a public meeting in Sheffield on New Year's Day 1874 that a voice in the crowd called out: 'What about Home Rule for Ireland?' By a fortunate chance, Chamberlain's answer was reported:

Home Rule for Ireland is worthy of a separate and lengthened discussion. I can only say now, generally, that if Mr Butt may be considered as a true exponent of the views of the Home Rulers, I am in favour of the system he advocates, and I believe also that the extension of the system of local government would be of the greatest advantage both to England and Ireland. It is only candid and fair to add that I am not in favour of any system which would go further than this, and which would separate the Imperial relation between the two countries.

The reference to Mr Butt's 'system' is highly significant. Isaac Butt (1813–79), MP for Harwich 1852, Youghal 1852–65 and Limerick 1871–79, appears to have invented the term 'Home Rule' and was leader of the Home Rule party from 1871. His 'system' was federal, as set forth in his book *Home Government for Ireland – Irish federation: its meaning* (1870). It is thus clear that at least as early as 1873 Chamberlain had reached the position of linking the Irish question with federalism and regarding a federal framework as the only acceptable condition of Home Rule.

The forgotten inventor of 'Home Rule': a portrait of Isaac Butt MP by J. B. Yeats (1839–1922), the father of the poet

THE **WIZARD** OF THE GAS.

A FEAT OF LE(D)GER-DE-(GAS)-MAIN

CHAPTER II

Mayor of Birmingham

It was in November 1873, shortly before the general election and his defeat at Sheffield, that Chamberlain was chosen mayor by the Liberal majority on the Birmingham town council. He almost immediately afterwards sold out his share in the screw business (which in later years became Guest, Keen & Nettlefold) in order, at thirty-seven, to devote himself exclusively thenceforward to public life. He plunged at once into a programme of municipal development, of which the three outstanding and characteristic features, in three successive years, were the municipalization of gas, the municipalization of water and the municipalization of redevelopment land in the centre of the town.

In 1873 Birmingham was backward, not to say barbaric, in comparison with other and smaller towns and cities in its physical appearance and its sanitary and social provision. Other cities were before Birmingham in the municipalization of public services. What was special about Chamberlain's onslaught was the dedication to managerial efficiency and to profitability. He advocated the civic acquisition of the right to supply gas not to spread the cost of supply across users and non-users, and not merely to give a civic impetus to improved and extended supply, but, by efficiency, to enhance the profit and lower the price while endowing Birmingham with a revenue-producing asset. The economies of scale, successfully exploited in making screws, were to be applied to the making and distribution of gas with public capital at purely nominal risk. The Mayor 'ran' gas and water as he had 'run' Chamberlain & Nettlefold: in fact, he offered, in the course of debate, to rent the gas undertaking from the corporation at £20,000 a year and guaranteed to make a personal fortune out of it by the time he was fifty.

Chamberlain derived the case for municipalization from the concept of monopoly: 'all monopolies *which are sustained in any way by the state*' – the qualification italicized would suggest itself

A cartoon of 1879 bears out the profit forecast by the former Mayor before municipalization

23

naturally to a non-statutory monopolist in screw-making – 'ought to be in the hands of the representatives of the people, by whom they should be administered and to whom their profits should go';[5] but there were ulterior motives, because local government was a good thing in its own right: 'I am inclined to increase the duties and powers of local authorities, and would do everything in my power to constitute them real local parliaments supreme in their special jurisdiction' – a formulation not without overtones of federalism (see pp. 21, 62), though there is nothing to suggest that the use of the word 'parliament' implied legislative powers.

When the turn of water came, and the Water Company was bought out by means of a private Act, a new turn was added to the theory, the Mayor securing the passage through the Council of a resolution that, 'whereas there should be a profit made on the gas undertaking, the water should never be a source of profit; all profit should go in reduction of the price of water.' I have found no evidence that Chamberlain examined the questions (1) why water but not lighting and heating should be provided at minimum price, (2) why profit-making was beneficial to the supply of gas but not of water, (3) on what principles the price of a supply by a statutory monopoly should be fixed – this last a question not answered by the reply that neither a loss nor a profit is to be made.

During the same parliamentary session of 1875 in which Birmingham secured its private Bill to municipalize the water supply, the Home Secretary, Richard Cross, and the President of the Local Government Board, George Sclater-Booth, in Disraeli's government, passed the Artisans' Dwellings Act,* which gave municipalities power to acquire compulsorily and to clear and redevelop areas of unsanitary housing and by which they were empowered to retain the freehold but not, without specific authority, to build houses themselves. Chamberlain was an enthusiast for the principle of the Act, and his co-operation with the two Tory ministers in shaping it and their goodwill towards his other municipal enterprises in Birmingham perhaps raised in his mind for the first time the unspoken question whether he could not, somehow and in some matters, work with and through the Conservative Party.

At all events, as soon as the Bill was law in July 1875, Birmingham put forward an 'improvement scheme' under it, which, as subsequently extended, would redevelop a great triangle of squalid housing between the two railway stations (New Street and Snow Hill) by driving through it a great new

Above: Birmingham housing at the time of the 'improvement scheme' – and since. *Below:* the private bill for the 'improvement scheme' was carried against the objectors in August 1876. The Birmingham cartoonist, G. H. Bernasconi, shows the Mayor on the footplate; the Council House in the background

* In full, the Artisans' and Labourers' Dwellings Improvement Act.

THE LOCAL OBSTRUCTIONISTS.

Joe (the Driver): "*Clear the track there now, if you don't want to be smashed.*"

Chamberlain's Corporation
Street, as it appeared in the
1890s from the New Street
end

commercial thoroughfare to be known as Corporation Street. It
was estimated that, after allowing for enhanced rateable value
and the commercial leases that would be obtained, the annual
burden on the rates would be only about £12,000 a year, and that
when the debt was cleared and the leases reverted in the twentieth
century, the Corporation would be an incalculably wealthy
landowner. Like gas and water, it was a commercial enterprise of
what Chamberlain called 'sagacious audacity'.[6] The private Bill
under which the financial and physical operations were carried
out during the decade to 1885 was passed in August 1876. Before
that, on 17 June, Chamberlain had entered the House of
Commons and his mayoralty ended in November, though he
continued an alderman; but from that day to this Corporation
Street – far more than the fountain-statue erected in 1880 in

26

Chamberlain Square next to the Town Hall – was to be his monument in the city with which his name was already synonymous.

There were in the area of the 'improvement scheme' 3,744 houses occupied by 16,596 persons. Despite the title and purpose of the enabling Act, therefore, and although Chamberlain in speech after speech dilated upon the horrific slum conditions and prayed in aid the moral as well as sanitary blessing of removing them, the scheme had little to do with the improvement of housing. It was all very well for him to say that 'unless we improve some of these dwellings off the face of creation, the labour of the minister of religion, the schoolmaster and philanthropist will be thrown away' or that 'by the work we are undertaking we hope to wrest from the fell grasp of disease and misery and crime whole populations which would be otherwise abandoned to them.'[7] In fact other less spectacular but more effective forces did the work.

In 1883 'some anxiety was manifested as to how far the convenience of the poorer classes had been affected by the removal of dwellings from the crowded streets in the centre of the town and also as to whether sufficient provision existed for the families who had been obliged to seek new places of abode.' The committee of investigation set up in consequence by the Council reported that 'there is adequate dwelling-house accommodation for the artisan and labouring classes within the borough', 8 per cent of all houses being unlet and the percentage being highest in the cheapest houses, the weekly rents of which were as low as 2s 6d. Overcrowding did not exist to any appreciable extent and with some exceptions 'the dwelling-house accommodation was found to be in a fairly sanitary condition.'[8] This explains why the Corporation 'had without success endeavoured to let sites for artisans' dwellings, there being so many dwellings of this kind unlet owing to overbuilding'.[9]

After he ceased to be mayor, Chamberlain was not quite finished with municipalization. He persuaded himself that a municipal monopoly of the liquor trade would be a profitable and practicable method of countering insobriety; and before the end of 1876 he was organizing a nationwide campaign for municipal public houses, based in part upon arrangements he had observed during a tour in Sweden. But the end of it was a private member's motion, thrown out in March 1877. By then Chamberlain's mind had made, at forty, the transition from municipal to national politics. The transition coincided with other changes.

Overleaf: Chamberlain's Birmingham in 1886

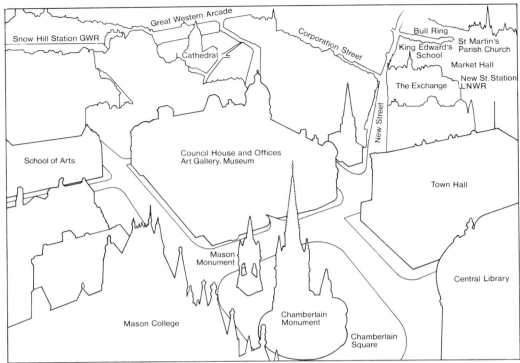

Key to the 1886 view of Birmingham

In February 1875 he became a widower for the second time. His second marriage, to Florence Kenrick, a cousin of his first wife Harriet Kenrick (to whom he was married 1861–63), had been exactly conterminous with his political life up to that time. Widowhood left him with a son, Austen, by his first wife, and another, Neville, by his second. Through the next thirteen tumultuous years of national politics and across the turning-point of his career, he was to live the existence of a single man.

Whether or not partly in consequence of his bereavement, the former Unitarian Sunday-school teacher seems at this period and lastingly to have admitted – at least to himself – that he was no longer a believer. It was within a year of his wife's death and in reference to it that he wrote the unmistakable though carefully guarded words in a letter to John Morley, the acknowledged and militantly agnostic editor of the *Fortnightly*, with whom he had become fast friends in the course of the Education League operations in 1873:

Does not the presence of this great grief in your household impress you with the cruelty of this life as you and I are compelled to see

The first two wives, the
Kenrick cousins, Harriet (died
1863) and Florence (died
1875): the baby is Neville
(born 1869)

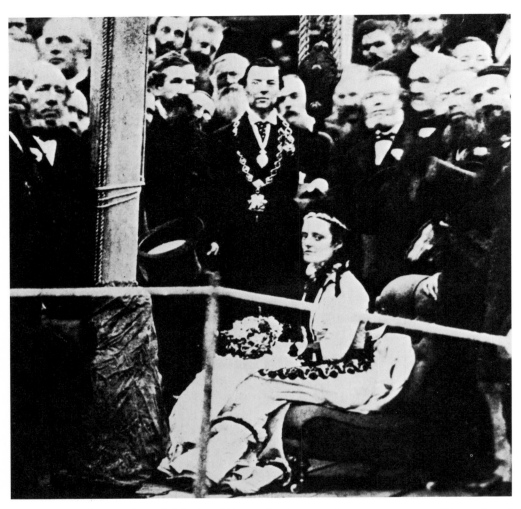

The Mayor lays the foundation stone of the new Council House (see p. 30 in the centre); his second wife already shows the approach of her fatal illness. The date is 17 June 1874

it? It is a hideous business, and our conception of its end and meaning is thoroughly unsatisfactory. We may be right – I fear we are – and I refuse to try and buy comfort by forcing myself into insincere conviction – but still I thoroughly abhor the result at which I have arrived, and I think it a grievous misfortune to have been born into such a destiny.

The religious was not the only mental change occurring. When, immediately after his election to parliament, Chamberlain went down with an attack of what was at last correctly diagnosed as gout, he made the obligatory jokes about the 'statesman's disease' and added: 'It is very painful, but will no doubt endear me to the Tories, to gain whose affection is now the chief object of my life.' It was of course three parts ironical – but not wholly, nor was the prophetic element, surely, altogether unconscious. There was more behind the words – and the thought – than the camaraderie with Disraeli's ministers which had developed over municipal enterprise or the bitter conviction that, if the Liberal Party under Gladstone was incapable of radical policies, less harm would come from a period of frankly Conservative government. There were aspects of Disraeli's administration – aspects that would be classified later as imperialist – which he positively approved.

The purchase of the Suez Canal shares by Disraeli, he writes – again to Morley – was 'wise' and 'plucky' and more than would have been expected of the Liberals if they had been in office, and it had paid dividends at once, in Abyssinia and in Egypt; for though 'it may or may not be desirable that we should have a finger in the Egyptian pie, we have got it'.[10]

So those were the private thoughts of the radical Mayor of Birmingham at the time he was piloting the Corporation Street improvement scheme through the Council and the Private Bill Committees!

CHAPTER III

In Parliament

It was June 1876 when the Mayor of Birmingham found his way into the 1874 parliament, at a by-election caused by the voluntary retirement of his old ally in the education battle, George Dixon. As was still not abnormal at that period, especially at by-elections, there was no contest.

Before the parliamentary recess he had got his maiden speech over – on an amendment to that 1870 Education Act which first brought him into national politics. When the House rose in August, Disraeli left it for another place as Lord Beaconsfield. More immediately important for Chamberlain, Gladstone made his unexpected and unheralded return from retirement, like some meteor re-entering the solar system, with his outburst against those Turkish atrocities in Bulgaria which were the prelude to the outbreak of the Russo-Turkish War in April 1877.

Within six months the new member for Birmingham had furnished the Liberal Party with a nationwide organization and its returned prophet and inspirer with the greatest political meeting of his life. When the next session of parliament opened, Chamberlain, with astonishing precocity and precision, took two large initiatives. In parliament he stood forth, along with Charles Dilke but otherwise virtually alone, as the defender and supporter of Gladstone's anti-Turkish stance in a House and a country where anti-Russian sentiment and bellicosity were sweeping all before them. When Russia went to war in April Gladstone insisted upon debating five anti-Turkish and pro-Russian resolutions, to the extreme embarrassment of the Liberal Party and his successor in its leadership, Lord Hartington. Only the Birmingham Radical had his heart in the fight and cheered on the Grand Old Man until, to his puzzlement, Gladstone suddenly withdrew – the tactical why and wherefore remaining obscure to however gifted a parliamentary novice who had not yet learnt to distinguish the shadow from the substance in House of Commons battles.

Gone to the House of Lords ('dead and buried, and in the kingdom of the blest'), Disraeli (Earl of Beaconsfield) is listened to by his ministers and other privy councillors from the Commons at the steps of the throne. The bishops' benches are exceptionally well filled

Gladstone inaugurates the
National Federation of
Liberal Associations in the
Bingley Hall, Birmingham,
31 May 1877

Meanwhile in February 1877 Chamberlain had carried out a
stroke long premeditated. The National Education League was
dissolved and its machinery and headquarters in Birmingham
placed at the disposal of a proposed new National Federation of
Liberal Associations, who were summoned to an inaugural
conference on 31 May in the Bingley Hall, Birmingham, to be
addressed as guest speaker by – of all people – Gladstone himself,
for whom willingness to gratify an ardent young paladin was
reinforced by a perception of the inherent possibilities, for
mischief and for power. The timing worked out perfectly. From
the parliamentary battle over his resolutions Gladstone proceeded to receive apotheosis from (allegedly) 'the largest
audience ever gathered together to hear a man speak', which
Chamberlain, elected its president, hailed from the chair as 'a real
Liberal parliament, outside the Imperial legislature and, unlike
it, elected by universal suffrage'.

For a man who had not yet been a year in parliament it was a
staggering achievement. The Liberal 'caucus' – a word, but not a
thing, borrowed from America – was in business, and the

circumstances were not visible when Frankenstein would have to wrestle for political survival against his creature.

The temperature of Gladstone's agitation fluctuated with the course of the Russian war on Turkey during the following twelve months. Chamberlain's enthusiasm sobered: 'past experience

Bernasconi (*cf.* p. 25) has transferred the theme of an earlier cartoon (*left*, Brougham and O'Connell) to Colonel Burnaby (see p. 20) and Chamberlain (*below*). The faithful Calthorpe is Sancho

The Liberal Opposition front bench in the Commons in 1878 (Bright, Gladstone, Harcourt, Hartington, etc.) listen to Sir Stafford Northcote. Chamberlain, followed by Dilke, seems about to sit down on the front bench; but that can hardly be

makes me very little sanguine of any real strength or union [against the moves towards war with Russia] being secured' (February 1877). He had parted even with Dilke over the issue, but was all the closer in Gladstone's counsels, with whom in April 1877 he was dining and having 'long conversations' every other day.[11] The end of it all came suddenly, when the diplomacy of Beaconsfield and Salisbury was triumphantly sealed by 'peace with honour' at Berlin in July.

That act was over; but another had opened before the end of 1878 with the colonial embarrassments in India and South Africa, which reversed the fortunes of the Conservative government. Gladstone and the Radicals were furnished with fresh and better supplies of the same sort of anti-jingo ammunition, which Chamberlain exploited in platform speeches throughout the country for the remaining life of the Parliament. But in the session of February to August 1879 Chamberlain found himself in new and unexpected company.

In February 1879 Dilke brought him into contact with Parnell, elected in 1875 for Meath, into whose hands the parliamentary struggle for Home Rule was passing from its originator, the ageing and gentlemanly Isaac Butt, for whom the harsh tactics

necessary to coerce the attention of parliament held little attraction. Dilke and Chamberlain found Parnell of the opinion 'that if the Liberals brought in a good [Land] Bill they would assure the good will of the Irish people and party for some years at least and might deal a fatal blow to the Home Rule movement'. If, then, the radical wing of the Party could get a 'good Irish Land Bill' inscribed on the Liberal banners, the rewards might be large.

Chamberlain and Parnell as they were when they first met in 1879. A most revealing study of Chamberlain

There were two subjects bulking large in the 1879 session which found Chamberlain and Parnell gaining for one another the cautious respect that grows up between members from widely separated political origins who find themselves fighting on the same side, especially against the feeling of their own parties.

The disaster of Isandhlwana, where the Zulus destroyed a British force on New Year's Day, 1879, was the first of the series of imperial humiliations that turned the glorious summer of Berlin into the winter of discontent in which Disraeli's administration drew to its close. The conduct and policy of the Zulu War became thereby one of the staple topics of the 1879 session. Chamberlain took a major part in support of Dilke in the censure of the government for retaining Sir Bartle Frere as High Commissioner after his ultimatum had provoked the unhappy war. His central argument was the unlimited consequences of the principle of seeking 'scientific frontiers' for the Empire and declining to tolerate 'strong neighbours':

We are undoubtedly the greatest colonizing nation on the face of the earth. Surely it is time for us to lay down clearly and plainly – to define accurately – the spirit and temper in which we are going to discharge the vast obligations which we have undertaken. Everywhere we hold territories acquired in the first instance by aggression and conquest; everywhere, with a reputation which I am sure was not calculated to secure the love of our neighbours, we come into contact with tribes more or less savage, more or less independent, more or less powerful; and everywhere our colonists call upon us to exert the whole force of this country to secure the proper subordination of those native tribes to the handful of Englishmen who claim the right to be supported by the whole power of the British Empire. I ask the House, where is this policy to stop? It seems to me, if it goes on as it has commenced, we shall have very shortly the whole responsibility of the government of South Africa on our hands, as well as of vast areas of country in other parts of the world.[12]

It was another of those premonitions – this time of the Jameson Raid (p. 108) – with which his earlier years were studded.

By now Parnell was engaged in the campaign of obstruction which he had developed almost since his entry into the House. It may have been as grist to that mill as much as for any other reason that he supported Chamberlain, as the Zulu War proceeded, in calling for safeguards against reprisals upon the Zulus for Isandhlwana:

When you make war against a savage nation, it follows that your soldiers will also become more or less savage; and when they see their own countrymen massacred, it is almost impossible to restrain them. Therefore Her Majesty's Government should be careful not to enter into a war with a savage people unless compelled by the most urgent necessity to do so.[13]

The operations of the Irish Home Rule members, like those of obstructionists before and since,* had in previous sessions already fastened upon the Army Discipline Acts. In the course of utilizing them, they brought and kept before the attention of parliament the question of flogging in the Army and were one of the elements in the House which made that among the principal topics of the second half of the session of 1879 in the context of a permanent Army Discipline Bill. In this they were joined by Chamberlain, who, in supporting abolition in preference to limitation, referred on 19 June[14] to obstruction and paid a

* E.g. the activities of Mr George (now Lord) Wigg in 1954.

marked compliment to Parnell:

If there is any threat in this House or out of it of anything like obstruction, we must not lose sight of the fact that the Government only made reasonable concessions after four days' discussion. In fact we can get nothing from the Ministry except by what is commonly called obstruction. Therefore the Ministry has no right to complain if opposition is carried further than previously we have been accustomed to carry it. . . . The friends of humanity and the friends of the British Army owe a great debt of gratitude to Mr Parnell for standing up alone against this system of flogging when I myself and other members had not got the courage of their opinions. The hon. member has opposed flogging in the Mutiny Bill, but unsuccessfully; he has opposed it unsuccessfully in the Prisons Bill; but now he raises it again, and I hope that his efforts will be crowned with success.

Eventually Chamberlain and other Radicals drove and goaded their reluctant front bench under Hartington to the point, after weeks of debate, of forcing them to propose an official motion on 17 July 1879 to abolish flogging for military offences. The motion was defeated by the government; but Chamberlain saw advantage for the Liberals in having joined the Irish in their parliamentary tactics. Though he had earlier[15] foreseen that the Irish would compel the House of Commons to defend itself against them by unwelcome procedural weapons, he was 'sure we are making a great mistake by helping to create a feeling against the Irish [on obstruction], which will all tell in favour of the Tories. They will pose as the friends of order, and get all the advantage of our denunciations of obstruction.'

The author Justin McCarthy, whose first parliamentary session was 1879, dictated a quarter of a century later[16] that

Sir Chas. Dilke and Mr. Chamberlain boldly and vigorously maintained Parnell in his policy of obstruction when it only professed to concern itself with Irish national questions. They identified themselves so closely with his Irish policy that it became a familiar joke in the House of Commons to describe Dilke and Chamberlain as the Attorney-General and the Solicitor-General of the Home Rule party. . . . Again and again I heard Mr. Chamberlain express his entire approval of the obstructive policy adopted by Parnell and declare that it was the only way by which Parnell could compel the House of Commons to give a hearing to Irish claims. . . . Dilke regarded Home Rule as an essential part of a federal system. . . . Therefore even if the Irish people had not been themselves awakened to the necessity for a home rule legislature in Ireland, Dilke would have been in favour of urging on them the advantages of such an arrangement. . . . Chamberlain was not so convinced an advocate of the general system of home rule as Dilke but he was always emphatic in his declarations that, if the large majority of the Irish people desired home rule, their desire should be granted to them by the Imperial parliament.

It seems likely that McCarthy's recollection had been greatly warmed and exaggerated by the lapse of time and his own aspirations. Nevertheless, if there was even a fraction of this relationship in 1879, it could have been one consideration which commended Chamberlain for elevation the next year.

The government knew, better than anyone out of office, how rapidly nationalist Ireland was becoming intractable. When Disraeli suddenly dissolved in March 1880, almost immediately after the opening of the new session, his letter to the Duke of Marlborough, which was the equivalent of an election manifesto, devoted itself almost exclusively to Ireland and the Union and made this the pre-eminent issue. The dissolution was taking place now because 'the measures respecting the state of Ireland, the relief Bills to deal with the failure of the harvest', were on the statute book. Despite the care, however, of the administration for 'the improvement of Ireland and the content of our fellow-countrymen in that island',

a danger, in its ultimate results scarcely less disastrous than pestilence and famine, distracts that country. A portion of its population is endeavouring to sever the constitutional tie which unites it to Great Britain in that bond which has favoured the power and prosperity of both. It is hoped that all men of light and leading will resist this destructive doctrine.

There are some who challenge the expediency of the imperial character of this realm. Having attempted, and failed, to enfeeble our colonies by their policy of decomposition, they may perhaps now recognise in the disintegration of the United Kingdom a mode which will not only accomplish but precipitate their purpose.

The theme of the Union* was thus linked with the theme of the Empire. The government was aware, as the public and the Opposition as yet were not, of the mounting threat of obstruction in parliament and violent agitation in Ireland. Gladstone denounced Disraeli's words as 'baseless and terrifying insinuations', and the Irish in English constituencies were exhorted by the Home Rule organizations to 'vote against Benjamin Disraeli as you would vote against the mortal enemy of your country and your race'. In the event, the Liberals were returned in the early days of April 1880 by a majority of more than fifty over Conservatives and Irish Home Rulers combined.

The year 1880; the sentiment impeccable

* W. F. Monypenny and G. E. Buckle (*The Life of Benjamin Disraeli, Earl of Beaconsfield*, 6 vols, 1910–20, vi. 510) have a tantalizing statement devoid of reference: 'Beaconsfield, there is reason to believe, was prepared to consider some sort of federal constitution for Ireland.'

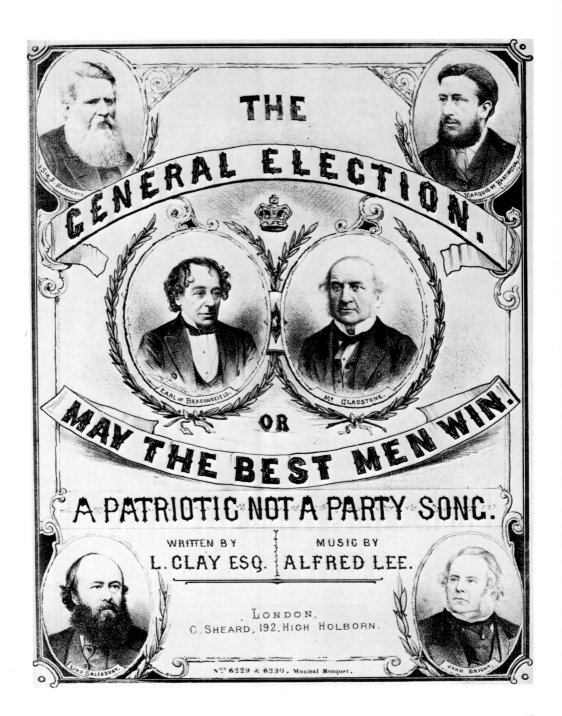

The Earl of K——

"The Right Hon. Gentleman walked over from the Home Office."

The Duke of Argyll's Successor

Prince and Lieutenant: the present Chief Secretary of Ireland

The Right Hon. J. B——

Lord N's morning Bailiff

Business

The Premier's Hats.

Before the Council: a peep into the Council Chamber

The Right Hon. Mr D——

The late Marquis and his dog Ponto

SWAIN sc

44

CHAPTER IV

Mr Gladstone's Government, 1880–85

After an election is won, the breathless days or weeks of government-making follow. Chamberlain and Dilke, like many rising and sympathetic young allies before and since, made a compact. Unless at least one of them was in the Cabinet, neither would join the government. Unlike many such another compact before and since, this one stood the strain. They transmitted their terms through Harcourt, the new Home Secretary. On 26 April Gladstone countered by offering Dilke junior office and merely hinting to him that Chamberlain might get the same. Nothing doing. The Prime Minister tried likewise with Chamberlain.* Nothing doing again. So the Prime Minister capitulated: he made Chamberlain President of the Board of Trade, and Dilke thereupon settled for Under-Secretary for Foreign Affairs.

As often, Gladstone may have been more worldly-wise than magnanimous. Junior though Chamberlain was, he had been largely instrumental in the Grand Old Man's comeback. Moreover, he controlled the effective Liberal machine and represented a huge radical following which would be more important still once the franchise, as foreshadowed, was extended. Better, then, in than out, caged than loose. So Chamberlain, less than four years in parliament, and less than forty-four years old, was a Cabinet minister, and that in a Cabinet, except for Bright and Forster, of Whig lords and commoners.

At this point I am compelled to resort to that device, most reprehensible in a historian, of deserting chronology so as to follow Chamberlain's career in the Cabinet, first of all leaving out Ireland, and then, over again, leaving out everything else. The necessity is that Ireland leads straight to the pivotal point of Chamberlain's life; the excuse is that Ireland largely was a thing apart and was so apprehended by the actors.

The crowd watches Gladstone's cabinet arrive at No. 10. Chamberlain, labelled 'Business', is in a hurry. Presumably Hartington's dog Ponto did not get beyond the anti-chamber

* The evidence for this item, unknown to history, is the otherwise unintelligible first sentence of Gladstone's subsequent letter of offer: 'Dear Mr Chamberlain – I have made progress since yesterday afternoon, and I may add there is a small addition to my liberty of choice beyond what I had expected' (27 April 1880). Gladstone could not have so written, had he had no previous communication with Chamberlain.

London. 7 July 1883

By his entry into the Cabinet Chamberlain was precipitated at once into the whole range of the political questions and decisions of the country and the Empire. A minister outside the Cabinet can, indeed must, concentrate above all upon his department; but a Cabinet minister has only the choice of being a nonentity or else applying his mind and his advice to every successive issue which comes before the government. For Chamberlain there was no question which it had to be. His abilities and personality apart, as representative of the radical element on which the government

Vincent Brooks Day & Son, Lith

Gladstone (why standing?) addresses a Cabinet of thirteen in the Cabinet room of today but at a smaller – and square – table. Chamberlain and Dilke sit together opposite him: 7 July 1883

and its majority depended, his voice had to be heard on every issue. Ironically, though he plunged, as every new minister does, with zest into the management and affairs of his own department, Ireland and the other great matters which demanded his attention denied the Board of Trade both parliamentary time and publicity for almost three years.

Gladstone's Colonial Secretary, Lord Kimberley, was in the Lords. By one of those premonitory strokes of fortune which occur at intervals along Chamberlain's path, he was nominated to be the

47

senior spokesman in the Commons. The Liberal Party had been opposed to the continued annexation of the Transvaal, none more than Chamberlain, albeit with the prophetic proviso 'unless some unforeseen circumstances lead to a large immigration of Englishmen'. When the government hesitated (for the sake of the 'natives') to act accordingly on entering office, he took the rebellious step of declining to vote against a private member's motion to reduce the High Commissioner's salary at the end of a debate on the policy of annexation.* After the military defeat inflicted by the Boers at Majuba Hill in February 1881, Chamberlain was one of those who enforced and defended the decision to give the Transvaal independence, though fatefully British suzerainty in external affairs was maintained.

The applause for Chamberlain's defence of withdrawal from the Transvaal in the House of Commons had scarcely died away in the summer of 1881 when it was renewed by his rebuttal of a motion warning against a 'reactionary and Protectionist' commercial treaty with France – another event which cast a long shadow forward. 'The people of this country', the mover** said, 'are beginning to ask themselves whether a policy of admitting without question whatever comes from abroad freely when our exports are heavily taxed in those countries is a sound and profitable one.' The peroration of Chamberlain's reply was stirring: 'A tax on food . . . would raise the price of every article produced in the United Kingdom and it would indubitably bring about the loss of that gigantic export trade which the industry and energy of the country, working under conditions of absolute freedom, has been able to create'; but the speaker's inner certainties did not match his language.

Dilke, in negotiation with a French Republic attempting to reverse the principles of the Empire's treaty of 1860 with Cobden, noted that Chamberlain 'held in a still stronger form' his own views in favour of retaliatory tariffs, for example on wine, counterbalanced by lower duties on Italian and *colonial* produce. A few months later Dilke reported his friend as 'arguing that there was a chance that some day there would be formed a British *Zollverein*, raising discriminating [*sic*] duties upon foreign produce as against that of the British Empire'. Chamberlain's horizons were expanding explosively; and in the winter of 1881–82 events in another quarter, Egypt, had opened to him other unexpected vistas.

When Arabi Pasha, through the Egyptian army, made himself master of the Khedive Tewfik and of Egypt at the end of 1881,

* 31 August 1880. The member was L. H. Courtney (Liskeard).
** The mover was none other than C. T. Ritchie, who was to resign from the Treasury twenty-two years later in opposition to the Conservative Cabinet's espousal of Chamberlain's tariff reform!

UNFAIR TRADE WINDS.

Chamberlain opposed the 'joint note' from Britain and France announcing that they would restore the Khedive's authority and thus secure the income of the European holders of Egyptian bonds; but when the Anglo-French fleet at Alexandria, unsupported by a landing force, produced anti-European riots there, Chamberlain supported the decision to bombard, upon which Bright resigned. That was 11 July 1882. The step once taken, an army was despatched which defeated Arabi at Tel-el-Kebir on 13 September and made Britain mistress of Egypt. Chamberlain told the House of Commons that it had been 'their duty to interfere, but for the sole purpose of putting down the

A premonition. As President of the Board of Trade, Chamberlain resisted the protectionist case ('fair trade'), illustrated with much the same cartoons as he was to use himself twenty years later (see p. 137)

In 1883 Chamberlain was already giving evidence of the independent radicalism which flowered in the 'unauthorized programme' of 1885. Hartington, Harcourt and others stay on shore

revolt and liberating the national sentiment'. In a public meeting at the end of the year, though still expecting that representative institutions would be established and Egypt evacuated in 'a year or two at the outside', he discovered that he had 'always protested in the strongest terms against the policy of non-intervention . . . and always thought that a great nation . . . could not wrap itself up in a policy of selfish isolation and say that nothing concerned it unless its material interests were directly attacked.'[17]

The session of 1883 was the first in which the Board of Trade at last got a serious share of parliamentary time. After slipping through a measure in 1882 permitting local authorities to municipalize, directly or in reversion, the generation of electricity, Chamberlain passed in parallel in 1883 both the Bankruptcy Act, giving the Board of Trade supervisory and administrative functions, and the Patents Act, creating a new Office for the cheap and efficient recording and protection of inventions. These were uncontroversial compared with the Merchant Shipping Bill of 1884, designed to prevent the scandalous over-insurance of unseaworthy cargo ships and thus reduce the high loss of life through wreck. Opposition was such that, working under the procedures of the day, so much more favourable to obstruction and delay, the Bill, not being central to the government's programme, was abandoned and reform had to wait for several years. Chamberlain at one point was with difficulty dissuaded by the Prime Minister from riding for a fall and resigning 'because, when Jonah had been thrown to the whale, the gale raised by the shipowners would abate'.

The class overtones of the opposition to the Merchant Shipping Bill had an unmistakable connection with the two other internal issues which – Ireland always apart – dominated Chamberlain's attention for the rest of the parliament. The debates on the Third Reform Bill, which extended household franchise to the counties, ran parallel to his Merchant Shipping Bill in the session of 1884. The attempt to exclude Ireland from it was defeated in May. In July the Lords rejected the Bill, on the ground that redistribution of seats must be simultaneous with extension of the franchise. Chamberlain launched into the 'peers against the people' campaign, with riotous meetings and personal exchanges of threats and ribaldries between himself and Lord Salisbury, and came near to demanding a fight to the finish with the Upper House. In the event a concordat on the basis of simultaneous redistribution and single-member constituencies enabled the reformed franchise to pass by the end of 1884.

The year 1885, correctly expected to be election year, opened with the first pronouncement of what was to be Chamberlain's 'unauthorized programme', an articulated and consecutive exposition of radical social objectives, which, as he was a Cabinet minister, could not but dictate the ground of the coming contest on the new franchise and constituencies. The instrument was a series of speeches at intervals of two or three weeks, which progressed from the 'ransom' that wealth ought to pay for security, to compulsory acquisition of land, manhood suffrage and graduated taxation. A Cabinet minister using this instrument is irresistible except by expulsion. How many other politicians who have made use of it since have assured their leaders retrospectively, as Chamberlain did Gladstone, and equally sincerely, that 'had it been possible for me to submit to you beforehand the speeches that I have recently delivered, I would readily have cancelled any part of them' (3 February 1885)? But, as both writers and recipients know, that is not the point. If the

By 1884 Chamberlain had
driven (pointed) screws
into the Cabinet with his Bills,
his radicalism and his caucus

speaker stays 'in', he will be master; and Chamberlain was still
'in' when a snap defeat of the government on a Finance Bill
amendment on 8/9 June 1885 ended the Liberal administration –
not without the sword of the Irish Nationalists thrown into the
scale.

It was, however, external events which gave the Gladstone
government its death wish; and the experience of those events had
worked a chemical change in Chamberlain's outlook on Britain
and the world, ever since 1883. They had, in a phrase, made him
a radical imperialist.

In 1883 Chamberlain had been among those who had been
profoundly moved by Seeley's *Expansion of England*. Indeed, it was
because Seeley's chair was at Cambridge that he chose that
university for his son Austen (born 1863). The rebellion of the
Mahdi had caught Britain still responsible for Egypt and
therefore for the Egyptian garrisons in the Sudan. It was to
organize their extrication that the government impulsively

The Prime Minister, *c.* 1883. The photograph contrives to convey what contemporaries found incomparably formidable. A man of 73

despatched Gordon, who was invested in Khartoum by March 1884. Then for five fatal months they shrank from the necessity of an expedition to rescue him, and when at last they recognized it, they decided upon a full-scale campaign under Wolseley which arrived two days too late, in January 1885.

The impression of this catastrophe, for which he bore his share of the responsibility, was deepened in Chamberlain by the simultaneous annexation by Bismarck's Germany of the Cameroons in July 1884 ('I was as much surprised as you were' – Lord Kimberley) and of New Guinea in December. It was on Chamberlain's insistence that the Boers were driven back out of Bechuanaland, into which they had infiltrated at the end of 1884; and a Cape politician, one Merriman, communicated to the world, through the *Pall Mall Gazette* for December, his prayer that before long Mr Chamberlain might become Secretary of State for the Colonies! It was an augury which Chamberlain is known to have noted.

CHAPTER V

Parnell

The ingredient artificially withdrawn from the narrative of Chamberlain's five years in Gladstone's Cabinet must now be replaced; for throughout those years, in parliament and in government, Ireland interwove itself with almost all the other events. The Irish thread in them has a curiously symmetrical pattern. A Coercion Bill for Ireland was awaiting the Liberal Cabinet on its entry into office; coercion fell to be renewed in the summer of 1885. Twice in the intervening five years Chamberlain entered into a negotiation at secondhand with Parnell to achieve what he supposed could be 'a final solution of the Irish problem', and twice, in circumstances which at the time cast doubt upon Parnell's good faith, the negotiation foundered.

The Liberal government allowed the Conservative Peace Preservation Act to expire on 1 June 1880, and proceeded to attempt to deal by conciliation with the Irish discontent which showed an agrarian face. A Compensation for Disturbance Bill, pushed through the Commons by Forster, the new Chief Secretary, with the warm approval of Chamberlain and Dilke, was thrown out in August by the House of Lords. Chamberlain proposed forthwith an extensive programme of public works, and under threat of resignation by Chamberlain and Dilke the Queen's Speech in January 1881, while calling for renewed and indeed intensified coercion, promised county boards and land reform. In Ireland the Land League and 'boycott' threatened the collapse of civil government; in parliament, as soon as it resumed, the Nationalists under Parnell destroyed by unprecedented obstruction the old conventions of the House of Commons. By the end of the session the Land Bill ('our message of peace to the Irish people' Chamberlain called it in a Birmingham speech) had passed into law; but its acceptance as such was the last thing desired by Parnell, who inflamed the agitation and violence and courted his arrest ('detention' in modern parlance) and committal to Kilmainham gaol on 13 October 1881.

After five days of debate on the motion to bring in the Protection of Person and Property (Ireland) Bill, Mr Speaker Brand on his own authority brought the debate to an end on 2 February 1881 by putting the question: the nineteen Irish members who voted against staged a violent protest
Overleaf: Gladstone introduces the Land Bill, 7 April 1881. Parnell is near the end of the third bench in the foreground. Gorst, Balfour and Lord Randolph Churchill (of the 'Fourth Party') are visible on the front bench below the gangway

54

MICHAEL DAVITT

It was thus that Parnell received O'Shea on 29 April 1882 and handed him the piece of paper which became the so-called 'Kilmainham Treaty'

He was released on parole, ostensibly to visit a dying relative, on 10 April 1882, and on 15 April, purporting to act on his behalf, the MP for Clare, Captain O'Shea, whose wife was Parnell's mistress and had already borne him a child, wrote to Gladstone and Chamberlain simultaneously proposing negotiation. Chamberlain sought and obtained Gladstone's and then the Cabinet's permission to proceed upon his personal responsibility. The outlines were rapidly agreed between O'Shea and Chamberlain: in exchange for a measure compulsorily extinguishing arrears of rent, Parnell would advise tenants to resume paying rent and would denounce all forms of lawbreaking. Declining an extension of parole, Parnell had returned to Kilmainham on 24 April: O'Shea visited him there and returned on 30 April to place in the hands of Chamberlain and Forster what purported to be a letter to himself from Parnell which was to be known as the 'Kilmainham Treaty'. It was placed before the Cabinet; Parnell and one or two other detainees were released unconditionally; and Forster resigned as Chief Secretary. He was replaced not, as some anticipated, by Chamberlain himself, but by the Financial Secretary, Lord Frederick Cavendish, who caught the next train to Dublin and on arrival was stabbed to death in Phoenix Park by a murder-gang.

His place was filled, after an offer to Dilke, by Sir George Trevelyan. The government, instantly reverting to coercion, introduced a drastic Crimes Bill the day after Lord Frederick's funeral, to be followed by an Arrears Bill. An amazing, and still unexplained, scene took place in the House of Commons on 15 May. When Gladstone declined to answer an Ulster member's demand to see the document or documents on 'the intentions of the recently imprisoned Members of this House with reference to their conduct if released from custody', Parnell rose and proceeded to read the 'Kilmainham letter'. Immediately Forster challenged its completeness. Parnell replied that he 'did not keep a copy of the letter in question' but that O'Shea had 'furnished him with a copy and it could be that one paragraph has been omitted'. O'Shea rose to make an explanation, but when he announced that 'I have not the document with me and am therefore unable to read it', Forster thrust his own copy into his hands and forced him to read it.

The letter as read by Parnell indicated that 'if the arrears question be settled upon the lines indicated by us, I have every confidence – a confidence shared by my colleagues [i.e. the other detainees] – that the exertions which we should be able to make strenuously and unremittingly would be effective in stopping outrages and intimidation of all kinds.' It went on to say that 'the accomplishment of the programme [of permanent legislation of an ameliorative character] would in my judgment be regarded by the country as a practical settlement of the Land Question, and I believe the Government, at the end of this session, would . . . feel themselves thoroughly justified in dispensing with further coercive measures.' It was into this last sentence that the version reluctantly read by O'Shea introduced the startling clause 'would, I feel sure, enable us to co-operate cordially for the future with the Liberal Party in forwarding Liberal principles'.

Inextricable confusion followed over the next forty-eight hours. In the course of it Forster disclosed O'Shea's communications with Chamberlain and himself, including a memorandum of their conversations; O'Shea astonishingly declared that he had written to Parnell his impressions 'of the debate on 26 April' – it was a Land Bill introduced by the Irish MPs themselves – and that 'in reply his hon. Friend wrote him the letter', dated Kilmainham, 28 April, 'which was read to the House';[18] and Chamberlain admitted that O'Shea had mentioned something about leaving a sentence out but that it had seemed to him unimportant and he had forgotten it. The only thing that is

The husband to be: Cornet O'Shea, 18th Hussars

reasonably clear is that O'Shea, whom of course Parnell could not disavow without severing his connection with Mrs O'Shea, had double-crossed everybody and that nobody emerged with any credit. Any 'solution' or 'message of peace to the Irish people' was blown to the winds.

However much Chamberlain might 'feel sure that England and Scotland would like a non-Irish session if we can keep the Irish quiet by fair words for the future',[19] two reforms in Great Britain were already beginning to cast their shadows as far as Ireland: the extension of the franchise and democratic local government. Since a similar extension could scarcely be withheld from Ireland, a large reinforcement of the Nationalist contingent was to be expected in any future parliament; and both Chamberlain and the Prime Minister were disposed to see in 'something more than county councils' – as previously in agrarian reform – the key to that problem which the extended franchise

The lover – at the husband's house (Parnell at Eltham)

would aggravate. However, these matters remained in abeyance – though Gladstone privately ruminated on 'some fundamental change in the legislative relations of the two countries'[20] – until in the session of 1884 the motion to exclude Ireland from the Third Reform Bill was defeated and the concordat of the autumn (p. 51) ensured that the Bill would pass and the number of nationalist votes in an overrepresented Ireland* would be trebled.

Something would need to be done, or at least commenced, in 1885, when the Crimes Act of 1882 was due to expire. Untaught by their experience eighteen months earlier, O'Shea and Chamberlain had frequent interviews in the autumn of 1884, and O'Shea implied that Parnell would consider a deal accepting minimum coercion in return for maximum local government. On 17 December 1884 Chamberlain addressed an injudiciously speculative letter to one Duignan, an Irish Liberal supporter in Walsall. 'I can never consent', he wrote, 'to regard Ireland as a

* Because of the dramatic fall in the population of Ireland after the 1840s, the island was increasingly overrepresented with the unchanged quota of seats allotted to it at the Union of 1800.

separate people with the inherent rights of an absolutely independent community.' On the other hand he would be willing to go further than 'county government' and 'transfer the consideration and solution of questions such as education and land which require local and exceptional treatment in Ireland and which cannot be dealt with to the satisfaction of the Irish people by an Imperial Parliament entirely to an Irish Board altogether independent of English government influence, which might also deal with railways and other communications and would *of course* be invested with powers of taxation in Ireland for these strictly Irish purposes.'

This was Home Rule with a vengeance. Not surprisingly it soon 'leaked' and began to find its way back to Gladstone and Chamberlain – first, in January 1885, as a set of proposals represented as emanating from Parnell as his price for eighty votes in a future parliament, if combined with an emasculated renewal of the Crimes Act; and later, in April 1885, as regarded by Cardinal Manning and the Irish bishops 'as satisfying all reasonable and just demands'. It is curious that in setting himself with Dilke to 'sell' this to a Cabinet where only Gladstone was favourably disposed, Chamberlain appears to have become for the time being oblivious of the question of parliamentary representation, which, as the guarantee of his postulated 'integrity of the Empire', he had already seen led to a federal United Kingdom (p. 21).

One cannot escape a suspicion that he was content to suppress this crux. In his letter to Duignan he wrote of his proposals as 'more congenial than that of bullying English officials and the *English House of Commons*, while the Imperial Parliament would continue to regulate for the common good the national policy of *the three kingdoms*'. The italics are mine, but the logic Chamberlain's. What such an 'Imperial Parliament' might be like must already have been in his mind when in the autumn of 1880 he and Bright were the only Cabinet ministers to support Gladstone's 'proposal to create Grand Committees for England, Ireland and Scotland'. Parnell too provided the counterpoint when he asserted:[21] 'We cannot under the British constitution ask for more than the restitution of Grattan's Parliament, but no man has the right to fix the boundary of the march of a nation.'

The Cabinet proved obdurate. Its disagreement was sealed by Gladstone's announcement on 15 May 1885 of the intention to renew coercion without proceeding at the same time either to a local government or a land purchase measure, and then, on 20

May, that there would be a Land Purchase Bill after all, but financed for one year only. Dilke resigned without waiting for Chamberlain, and Chamberlain fulfilled their compact by following suit; but while the resignations remained in suspension, the defeat on the Finance Bill in the early hours of 9 June ended the government's life. Parnell had taken forty of his followers into the Conservative lobby, and seventy-six Liberals had failed to vote. Gladstone pronounced both epilogue and prologue when he told Hartington he was 'firmly convinced that on local government for Ireland [Chamberlain and Dilke] hold a winning position. You will all, I am convinced, have to give what they recommend – *at the least what they recommend*.'

In July the last item of the 'unauthorized' radical programme was published in the *National Review*. Largely the work of a Dublin solicitor, George Fottrell, it was entitled 'Local government and Ireland' and comprised a scheme of national councils for each constituent nation of the United Kingdom. Federation was back.

The woman in the locket: 'Kitty' O'Shea in 1880. The picture which Parnell always carried

63

64

CHAPTER VI

The Hinge

'Unmuzzled' by the break-up of the government, Chamberlain pronounced in a series of speeches in June and July 1885 the message of local government and devolution, now coupled explicitly with 'Home-Rule-all-round'.

I am already [11 June] contemplating a campaign to be opened in Scotland in favour of my proposals for local government and the settlement of the Irish question. . . . They will appreciate the arguments by which I shall justify its application to Scotland as well as to other portions of the United Kingdom.[22]

In pursuance of the scheme Chamberlain and Dilke planned an Irish tour. The rebuff which they received from 'Parnell's paper', *United Ireland*, and from the Roman hierarchy opened their eyes to what they should not have needed telling. Though the Conservative government of Lord Salisbury was only a brief caretaker, it declined to enact the Liberal coercion measure and under Lord Randolph Churchill's influence showed an open mind towards the ideas of devolution which had been canvassed. Not only were the Conservatives the 'government in being' – Parnell paid a private call to the new Lord Lieutenant, Carnarvon – but who knew but that the influence of the now reinforced Nationalists during the election and eighty Nationalist members after it might put a captive Conservative government into office and exact from it a more extensive Home Rule than Chamberlain had ever been prepared to contemplate?

Chamberlain and Dilke were out on a limb, and the matter had to be settled one way or another before the coming election. It was May 1882 all over again. On 11 July Chamberlain demanded through O'Shea a 'full and frank reply' from Parnell, intimating that 'I believe that the next election will in any case give a majority to the Liberal party independently of any Irish support and if the offer now made on behalf of the English Radicals is rejected, I cannot see any light in the future.' Parnell's silence was the eloquent reply. On 29 July O'Shea conveyed to him Chamberlain's message that 'the Liberal leaders who had

Celebrities of today and yesterday, 1886 – a composite photograph. Key on p. 154

adopted your proposal to them and who had run much risk in promoting the adoption of it, must now drop it from the programme.' In the interval between the two communications had occurred the accusation of adultery which destroyed Dilke. Chamberlain would fight the election alone – on the 'unauthorized programme'.

The long-drawn-out nationwide pre-election campaign of speeches opened for Chamberlain at Hull at the beginning of August and ended at Birmingham in the latter part of October. Early in the course of it the rupture between the Irish Nationalists and the Radicals was publicly declared by blow and counterblow exchanged between Parnell, who at Dublin on 24 August declared for 'national independence', and Chamberlain, who at Warrington on 8 September denied the nationhood of Ireland and reaffirmed his federalist thesis: 'I cannot admit that five millions of Irishmen have any greater inherent right to govern themselves without regard to the rest of the United Kingdom than the five million inhabitants of the metropolis. . . . I for my part would concede the greatest measure of local government to the Irish people as I would concede it also to the English and the Scotch.'

Chamberlain proved to be mistaken in his anticipation of the outcome of the election, in which polling began on 24 November. By early December it was clear that the Liberals would have exactly as many seats as the Conservatives and Home Rulers combined. The result owed something to the fact that at the crucial moment, on 21 November, Parnell had thrown the weight of his influence against the Liberals by calling on Irish electors in Great Britain to vote them out.

On the other hand, the outcome of the election weakened Chamberlain's personal position, temporarily at least, because the 'unauthorized programme' appeared signally to have failed to 'bring home the bacon'. 'The Liberals', said *The Times* on 26 November, 'have to thank Mr Chamberlain not only for their defeat at the polls but for the irremediable disruption and hopeless disorganization of the party'; and it was in vain that Chamberlain, in a speech at Leicester on 3 December, claimed that the losses had occurred because the election had *not* been fought on his programme.

Given the normally superior 'whipping' of a government party and the imperfect attendance of Irish MPs, the result meant that, if they turned out Salisbury's caretaker government, the Liberals would be able to govern, but only on a knife-edge, in constant peril of losing their majority on any occasion when the Conservatives and Home Rulers made a special and united effort, and faced with an intensification of the novel and little understood experience of systematic parliamentary obstruction. As Chamberlain had made it plain in his campaign that he would not enter a Liberal government uncommitted to free schools, graduated taxation and compulsory acquisition of land by local authorities for allotments and small holdings, so he had resolved not to enter into competition for Mr Parnell's support on his terms for a separate and independent parliament (Warrington). But he was not the only one to have decided what to do if the Liberals could govern only with Parnell's support.

Already in the summer Gladstone had been in tentative contact, through his son Herbert and through Mrs O'Shea, with the elusive Parnell. If he needed Parnell's support it would cost much more than Chamberlain's limit: it would be the whole Parnellite hog. In the autumn, after the strange episode of a Chamberlain visit at Hawarden, he was telling Chamberlain that 'an instinct blindly impresses me with the likelihood that Ireland may shoulder aside everything else.' Chamberlain, still blinkered by his conviction of a Liberal majority, could only hark back to his 'National Councils' plan and opine that 'the only chance is to let the Irishmen "stew in their juice"' and that 'if we have a good majority it may be possible to divide them and secure some support for our proposals.'

The Grand Old Man's instinct now turned out to have been right. Chamberlain's hopes were cobwebs: the alternatives were either to leave the Conservatives to compromise themselves with Parnell, if so minded, and then, when the Conservatives fell and the Liberals had to replace them, to struggle along unaided but with increasing procedural protection against obstruction – or else to govern *with* Parnell on Parnell's terms.

Gladstone was for the second course, and a press 'leak' from Herbert on 17 December informed the country that 'with safeguards for the unity of the Empire, the authority of the Crown and the supremacy of the Imperial Parliament' his father 'was prepared to take office with a view to the creation of an Irish Parliament to be entrusted with the management of all legislative and administrative affairs, securities being taken for the representation of minorities and for an equitable partition of all imperial charges'. Gladstone might announce that 'the statement is not an accurate representation of my views and is, I presume, a speculation upon them'; but from that moment there could be no

The humiliation of Gladstone's brief government of January to June 1886, held at the price demanded by the Irish Nationalists, was gleefully commemorated in cartoons long after. These two, entitled 'The Parnellite Bath' and 'The Turn-Coat Government', were produced after Sir G. O. Trevelyan, shown among the penitents, had got back to parliament in August 1887 for Bridgeton, Glasgow, after ejection from the Border Burghs in 1886.

substantial doubt of Gladstone's mind, and nothing could ever again be as it had been.

It would be surprising if Gladstone, faced with the prospect – not for the last time – of governing with Irish votes, had not noted the consequences of a form of Home Rule so drastic as to eliminate Irish representatives from Westminster. In Great Britain alone the Liberal Party still had a heavy majority. This may have been among the motives which led Gladstone to frame the legislation initially upon the basis – logically indefensible, if the Union was to continue at all – that there would be no Irish MPs in the House of Commons (see p. 8).

For the moment, unlike Hartington, who on 21 December publicly came out against Home Rule, Chamberlain 'lay low'; but in private letters over Christmas he made his unchanged position clear to old Radical associates, such as Labouchere and Morley, who were rallying to Hawarden. Home Rule, except in a federal frame, was separation:

There is only one way of giving *bona fide* Home Rule, which is the adoption of the American Constitution.

1. Separate legislature for England, Scotland, Wales and

possibly Ulster. The three other Irish provinces might combine.

2. Imperial legislature at Westminster for Foreign and Colonial affairs, Army, Navy, Post Office and Customs.

3. A Supreme Court to arbitrate on respective limits of authority.

. . . There is a scheme for you. It is the only one which is compatible with any sort of Imperial unity, and once established it might work without friction.

Or again, to Morley, 'I do not believe that there is anything between National Councils and separation.' He was even prepared to contemplate actual separation, rather than the ambiguous worst-of-all-worlds:

If we are to give way it must be by getting rid of Ireland altogether and by some such scheme as this: call Ireland a protected state; England's authority to be confined exclusively to the measures necessary to secure that Ireland shall not be a *point d'appui* for a foreign country. . . . The worst of all plans would be one which kept the Irishmen at Westminster while they had their own parliament in Dublin.

Lord Salisbury's government met the new parliament on 21

January with a Queen's Speech containing a slap in the face to Parnell: 'I have seen with deep sorrow the renewal of the attempt to excite the people of Ireland to hostility against the legislative union between that country and Great Britain. I am resolutely opposed to any disturbance of that fundamental law, and in resisting it I am convinced that I shall be heartily supported by my Parliament and my people.' As if that were not enough, the Speech went on to foreshadow a new Coercion Bill, which followed promptly on 26 January, while the Address was still being debated. That settled the matter. The government were turned out the same day on an amendment to the Address dealing not with Ireland but, advisedly, with allotments and small holdings. In the division the Nationalists of course voted against the government; but several eminent Liberals, among them Hartington, supported it against their own party.

Within a few days Gladstone, having the Queen's commission, was offering Chamberlain a seat in a Cabinet to which Hartington would not belong. Offered the Admiralty, Chamberlain preferred – significantly (p. 53) – the Colonies, but settled for the Local Government Board, not without a kind of written treaty between Gladstone and himself. On his part Gladstone foreshadowed an intention to 'examine whether it is practicable to comply with the desire widely prevalent in Ireland for the establishment by statute of a legislative body to sit in Dublin and to deal with Irish as distinct from Imperial affairs in such a manner as to be *just to each of the three Kingdoms*'. On his side Chamberlain promised to give 'unprejudiced consideration to any proposals that may be made' while being assured of 'unlimited liberty of judgment and rejection on any scheme that may ultimately be proposed'.

Chamberlain promptly busied himself with a Local Government Bill to create county, district and parish councils, with powers of licensing, land acquisition and administration of local charities, and at Gladstone's request he circulated in the middle of February a scheme for Irish land purchase administered by an elected central board. It was a different Land Bill, involving £120 million to buy out the landowners, which Gladstone at last placed before the Cabinet on Saturday 13 March. Chamberlain immediately asked what form of authority was envisaged as guaranteeing the repayment, and when Gladstone referred to 'a separate Parliament with full powers to deal with all Irish affairs', Chamberlain sent in his resignation but was persuaded to withhold it in anticipation of the details of the Home Rule Bill, enquiring through Harcourt whether it was 'possible to discuss the matter on the basis of four bodies resembling the States governments in the United States'.

It was still the federal solution to which Chamberlain, as before and afterwards, consistently recurred. The temptation to interpret it as a dialectical *ad absurdum* is almost overpowering, but must be resisted. There is nothing in anything which Chamberlain said or wrote – and he was candid to a fault – that suggests he so regarded it or that it was so interpreted by any of those to whom the proposition was addressed. The fact has to be faced that in the penultimate decade of the last century a federal Britain or British Empire appeared at least arguable, not to say practicable. Britain had created federal states in Canada and Australia, and the case of America was ever-present; but it is difficult to resist the suspicion that the federal empires of the continent, above all the German Reich of 1871, had worked deeply if silently on the minds of British politicians. The idea was to play a large part in Chamberlain's subsequent life.

The final break came with Gladstone's declaration to the Cabinet and Chamberlain's cross-questioning on 26 March (p. 8). By a fortunate chance A. J. Balfour recorded[23] a dinner conversation with Chamberlain on the eve of that Cabinet which reveals how he foresaw the electoral revolution that must follow if Gladstone failed to carry the Home Rule Bill. 'Whether we like it or not', said Chamberlain, 'the Tories are in a minority in the country and it is only by the help of the Radicals that anything material can be done. . . . the condition of it being done successfully is that the whole affair should not be supposed to be a Tory–Whig manoeuvre.' To the view that 'at this moment if you were to poll the northern counties, you would find a majority of Home Rulers', which seemed to Balfour a 'prospect dark indeed', Chamberlain rejoined, most characteristically, that 'part of my democratic faith is that if a scheme is truly absurd (and, unless we are all in a dream, this scheme is so) people can be made to understand its absurdity'.

The alliance would, if Chamberlain could have it so, be with the Tories, not the Whigs: 'The Tory policy I understand with regard to Ireland. The Tories go in for coercion. I believe that if that could be carried out consistently for five years, it would succeed.' No wonder that Balfour reported to his uncle, Lord Salisbury, that 'we shall find in Chamberlain, so long as he agrees with us, a very different kind of ally from the lukewarm and slippery Whig, whom it is so difficult to differ from and so impossible to act with.'

CHAPTER VII

Towards the Tories

On the morrow of Gladstone's historic oration moving for leave to bring in a Bill 'to amend the provision for the future government of Ireland', Chamberlain made what was in effect his resignation speech. It was not a success as a speech, and at several points he found himself caught in embarrassments which suggest that for some reason he was ill prepared; but it 'won the continued plaudits of the Tory Party'.[24] He retorted upon those who argued that coercion was the only alternative to such proposals as Gladstone's, that these too would have to be imposed by coercion upon the Protestant population, 'prosperous and industrious and enterprising', constituting at least one-fifth of the population of an island comprising 'not a homogeneous community but two nations, two races and two religions'. On the other hand he recognised that the proposals had rendered obsolete his past projects of local government and national councils; and he pointed once more to a federal United Kingdom as the only means of satisfying the essential requirement of Irish representation in the Imperial Parliament. He even referred to the existence 'between the Colonies and this country' of 'a general desire to draw tighter the bonds which unite us and to bring the whole Empire into one federation' – the illusion which was to haunt his mind and dog his steps for the remainder of his life – but in subsequent debate he writhed under the gibes of those who pointed out that the radical programme (see p. 63) had dismissed federation as 'outside the range of practical politics' because it 'would involve so great a disturbance of the English Constitution'.[25]

Chamberlain had evidently pondered the meaning of federation deeply: an article, 'A Radical View of the Irish Crisis', in the *Fortnightly Review* of February 1886, the authorship of which he never disavowed, proved this. In particular he understood

At the turning-point of his political life, aged 50

that, by involving a written fundamental constitution, federation was incompatible with the continuance of the prescriptive elements – the hereditary House of Lords and above all the Monarchy ('it is hardly conceivable that even the nominal authority of the Crown could be long preserved'). The conclusion was dismal:

> The scheme involves the absolute destruction of the historical constitution of the United Kingdom, the creation of a *tabula rasa* and the establishment thereupon of the United States constitution in all its details. According to this precedent Ireland might have one or even two local legislatures, if Ulster preferred to retain a separate independence. Scotland and Wales would each have another, and England would also have a Parliament and a Ministry of its own. There would be over all an Imperial Parliament, charged entirely with the control of foreign and colonial affairs, military and naval expenditure, and customs and Post Office. It may be that such a proposal would not be seriously objected to by consistent Radicals, and it is probable that it would work without friction and preserve a real union of the Empire for defensive and offensive purposes; but it is hardly conceivable that the people of Great Britain as a whole are prepared for such a violent and complete revolution.

With such a bleak conclusion, advocating in practice no more than radical land reform in the forlorn hope of undermining Parnell's ascendancy, was Chamberlain to go out into the cold against Gladstone's Bill. Stripped to its essentials his motive was the instinctual defence of the historical unitary constitution. He was a Unionist.

Knowing the destructive logical implications of continued representation of Ireland in parliament, Chamberlain proceeded nevertheless to make that his condition for allowing a second reading to the Bill, because he foresaw that it would involve in committee demands for 'a separate assembly for Ulster, complete subordination of the Irish Assemblies to the Imperial Parliament', their power to deal 'only with subjects expressly referred to them', and the reversal of financial arrangements so that a mere block grant was paid over to the devolved administrations.[26]

It was the same test which divided the Liberal Party in the country. On 21 April Chamberlain's 'Two Thousand', the Birmingham caucus, passed a resolution demanding 'that the Irish members shall be retained at Westminster'. When this was defeated in the national caucus on 5 May, the headquarters of the National Liberal Federation was moved to London and a new Liberal Unionist Association was formed.

Faced with the prospect of some ninety Liberal defections Gladstone wobbled and equivocated to the last moment. Then he moved the Second Reading on 10 May offering no more than to 'give an unprejudiced ear [in committee] to proposals which others may make for the purpose of insuring the continued manifestation of common interest between Great Britain and Ireland in Imperial concerns'.[27] He had previously cited giving Irish members 'an opportunity of appearing in the House to take a share in the transaction' of an alteration in Customs and Excise!

Once more, as the debate wore on, the Old Master tried the trick of riding two horses at once; one day he suggested to a Liberal Party meeting that the Bill, if read a second time, could be withdrawn and introduced re-cast – only to repudiate any such notion on the floor of the House the next day. In the division, which took place after the twelfth day of debate on 7 June, 93 Liberals voted against Gladstone and the Bill, which was defeated by 30. John Bright, who was openly opposed both to Home Rule and to federation, voted against; and his letter intimating that he would do so was believed to have been a potent influence on the Radicals.

Gladstone dissolved. The election which followed gave the Conservatives a majority of 118; but 74 of those were Liberal Unionists, roughly half-and-half Whig and Radical. The balance

Despite Schnadhorst (p. 20) and other Liberal chiefs in the background, Chamberlain carries the Birmingham caucus of 2000 with him on butchering Gladstone's Irish bills

had departed from Parnell for ever and from the Irish Nationalists for a quarter of a century, and was now held by the Liberal Unionists, a fact which Lord Salisbury shrewdly recognised by advising the Queen to send for Lord Hartington, who declined. This is a situation in which the gaoler easily becomes the prisoner of his charges. There is nothing like keeping another political party in office by one's votes for giving one a sympathetic and almost protective understanding of their character and motives. After all, from division to division one is responsible for their remaining in office; and unless they are speedily to be turned out, one needs to defend the measures which they propose and for which, tacitly or formally, they must have reasonably assured themselves of one's support.

It might appear that the Liberal Unionists could as easily gravitate back to their Liberal matrix. In reality there was no such freedom of choice. Only those incompatible to the core with Conservative ministers, who found themselves almost accidentally in the Unionist boat, would peel off and rejoin Gladstone. For Chamberlain by now and, had he known it, long before there was no such incompatibility. In vain did the Liberal Unionist privy councillors persist in sitting on the Opposition front bench with the Gladstonians. In vain did Chamberlain advise Hartington that 'our real policy is never to vote with the Tories unless they are in danger and to vote against them whenever we can safely do so' (9 September 1886). The nub of the matter was in his words in the confidence debate on the Queen's Speech: 'I shall do nothing to turn out the Government so long as the Government which would take its place is committed to a separatist policy.' That would be, in effect, for the rest of his lifetime.

A brief episode at the end of 1886 provided corroboration. A combination of the Christmas spirit and of Lord Randolph Churchill's Lucifer-like resignation as Chancellor of the Exchequer – which seemed to portend an incompatibly reactionary Conservative stance – led to three 'Round Table' meetings between Chamberlain, Trevelyan, Morley, Harcourt, Herschell and Fowler, with Gladstone's knowledge if not approval. They served only to reaffirm Chamberlain's immovable insistence on 'Home-Rule-all-round' or none at all and on 'separate treatment of Ulster or part of Ulster'. His belief, expressed in a Christmas speech at Birmingham, that 'without solving the land question, Home Rule is impossible, and I believe that if you solve it Home Rule will be unnecessary' was as stubborn as it was purblind. The 'Round Table' ended in public recrimination.

The 'lost leader': Lord Randolph Churchill (*cf.* p. 56) about the time that he and Chamberlain were new members

In the session of 1887 the Liberal Unionists supported Conservative coercion measures in Ireland; but Chamberlain's pressure secured not only an Allotments Bill with compulsory powers but an Irish Land Bill providing, against Conservative instincts, for the reassessment and reduction of rents already judicially assessed. Even so, there was a near disaster at the end of the session when the government declared membership of the Irish National League to be criminal; of 69 Liberal Unionists, 47 under Hartington voted with the government, 5, with Chamberlain among them, against, and 17 abstained.

At about the same time Chamberlain came to the conclusion that his firmly held federal solution for Ireland was on both sides a non-starter and undertook to Hartington to consign it to silence henceforward. He was speaking that summer in Birmingham

Chief Commissioner for settlement of the fisheries dispute in Washington. On Chamberlain's right is Bayard, the American Secretary of State

when the following sentences escaped him: 'We shall be taunted, I suppose, with an alliance with the Tories. At least our allies will be English gentlemen.' There is no surer guide to what is happening below the surface, perhaps below the surface of consciousness, than words struck out in anger. Meantime two great political lubricants were applied: time – and patronage. The week after Chamberlain's vote against the government Salisbury offered him the post of Chief Commissioner in the United States for the settlement of the fishery dispute between the two countries. He accepted immediately.

In the three months November 1887 to February 1888 were negotiated a treaty, repudiated after the following presidential election, and a provisional protocol which lasted, controlling the access of New England fishermen to Canadian territorial waters: but a speech which Chamberlain made in Toronto was more important. 'It may yet be', he declared, 'that the federation of Canada may be the lamp lighting our path to the federation of the British Empire. It is an idea to stimulate the patriotism and statesmanship of every man who loves his country.' The note was

Bringing his bride home to a Birmingham civic reception, Christmas 1888

78

The house called Highbury, from the lawns

not new. The instance of Canada had been invoked by federalists in the Home Rule conflict of 1885–86 and imperial federation had been mentioned more than once; but at Chamberlain's point of transition from an old life to a new one it was understandable if the will-o'-the-wisp of a federal United Kingdom was magnified and transformed into the Brocken Spectre of a federal worldwide Empire.

The newness of Chamberlain's life thereafter was sealed by his third marriage. Before he left America he had become engaged – secretly until after the presidential elections – to a girl of twenty-four, less than half his age, a Miss Mary Endicott, daughter of the Secretary of War and a descendant of a governor of Massachusetts who had excised the cross of St George from the flag with his own hand. He returned to America to marry her at the end of the year and brought her to Highbury for Christmas 1888. The GCB was offered and declined, but the freedom of Birmingham accepted, an occasion for John Bright's last public speech in which he described imperial federation as 'a dream and

With the third Mrs Chamberlain, 1888

81

an absurdity' – words which provoked Chamberlain to enter into a little detail shortly after:

We should seek and find a concerted system of defence. The difficulty in the case of commercial union is much greater. It is hardly to be hoped that the protected interests, fostered by their system, will willingly surrender the privileges which they now enjoy. All we can do is to wait until proposals are made to us, and to accept them if they do not involve the sacrifice of any important principle or of any interest vital to our population.[28]

However veiled the language, there is no mistaking the meaning. This is not federation: this is customs union at the outside, but mutual protection or 'fair trade' at the minimum.

The political yeast of Chamberlain's situation as at once the patron and prisoner of the Conservative government which he kept in office worked with steadily increasing vigour as the life of the 1886 parliament lengthened. When the general election came – it would be later rather than sooner, with the by-elections going, as they did, consistently and sometimes disastrously against the government – on whose side would he fight? At a general election now the commitment must be unambiguous and could not, as in 1886, be subsumed under a single subject. Such a prospect casts its shadow far before. In Birmingham in 1888 a new-made Birmingham Liberal Unionist Association had to replace, and partly cannibalize, the old Liberal caucus, against the day when it would be needed to ensure – what? That no Gladstonian Liberal would be returned for a Birmingham constituency, municipal or parliamentary. Some of the candidates would be Conservatives – one of the members (H. Matthews in Birmingham East) was a Conservative already – and why should not the electors, and as many as possible, be Tories, of the 'Tory democracy' which Lord Randolph Churchill had once proclaimed in Birmingham itself? Gone were the days when Chamberlain cared to delight an audience by declaring that if a genuine 'Conservative working man' could be found, he ought to be stuffed and preserved in a glass case like a unique zoological specimen.

When the day of reckoning came, Chamberlain had to be able to show that the Conservative Party which he would seek to retain in office was by record as well as programme reasonably consistent with the causes with which he had always been identified – indeed, was arguably more so than Gladstone had proved. In every session after 1887 Chamberlain could note steady, though not unqualified, progression towards that

necessary objective. In 1888 the Conservative government established elected county councils in Great Britain: Chamberlain was able to secure that they contained no non-elective element, though he could not insist on the simultaneous application of the same measure to Ireland nor on the simultaneous creation of elective district and parish councils nor on full control by the county councils over the police. Still, it was a great measure, and one which had eluded Liberal governments.

The year 1889 was an *annus mirabilis* of screeching crises, which lifted the Home Rulers up to the skies and dashed them down again. Since April 1887 Parnell had lived under the cloud of the publication by *The Times* of letters purporting to be in his handwriting condoning the Phoenix Park murders of 1882 ('Parnellism and Crime' was the celebrated headline). In February 1889 a Judicial Commission exposed the letters as forgeries – Pigott the forger fled to Madrid and committed suicide there – and Parnell was the hero of the day. On Christmas Eve 1889 O'Shea filed a petition for divorce and cited Parnell as co-respondent. A year later, in November 1890, the undefended case was heard and the Irish party which Parnell had led

The Irish labourer, thanking Parnell for security of tenure, owed more to the Conservative agrarian measures. The caption: 'Whoever may forget you, I and mine shall always remember you gave us a home'

Parnell is re-elected leader of the Irish Party on 25 November 1890 in Committee Room 15, where ten days later the majority were to reject him

disowned him, to die only a few months after in Mrs O'Shea's arms.

A. J. Balfour as Chief Secretary had set himself to match coercion with a series of measures, in accordance with Chamberlain's diagnosis, to transform the agrarian condition of Ireland. These began to come to fruition in 1889 and 1890 with programmes of public works and a Land Purchase Act, though not yet accompanied, as Chamberlain would have wished, by elective local government responsible for its administration. The decisive step, however, was in 1891, when Goschen's Budget provided for free education both in board schools and denominational schools. Chamberlain had gained his point of twenty years before, though at the price of accepting and defending as permanent the so-called 'dual system' of secular and denominational schools side by side (p. 18). As for disestablishment, he was content formally to treat that item of the radical creed as a 'dead duck'.* For the rest, he could claim that, with a Small Holdings Act, embodying compulsory powers, in the final, pre-election session of 1892, the inspiration and support of Liberal Unionism had secured from the Tory Party the

* 'Now I find the active section of Nonconformists more fanatical, more bitter, more selfish and more unscrupulous than I have ever known the champions of the Church to be.' Letter to Rev R. W. Dale, 2 March 1891, quoted *EHR* (1962), p. 65.

acceptance and substantial realization of the programme for which, to Gladstone's discomfort, he had contended as a Radical ex-Cabinet minister at the fateful election of 1885.

In 1891 a joint conference of Liberal Unionists and Conservatives met in the Birmingham Town Hall; and when Lord Salisbury attended the Conservative National Conference in that same town hall in November, Chamberlain sat by his side and proposed the toast of 'the Unionist cause'. 'I neither look for nor desire', he said, 'reunion' with the Liberal Party. The transition was complete. When Hartington at last became Duke of Devonshire a few days later, his successor as Liberal Unionist leader, unanimously (as he insisted) acknowledged, was Joseph Chamberlain.

Chamberlain's senior partner: the Marquess of Salisbury

With an election now in the offing, Chamberlain began to prepare a mirror image of the campaign of 1885 (p. 51), whereby his speeches would provide his Conservative allies – and his Whig allies in the Liberal Unionist Party – with a radical programme, whether they liked it or not, fit to match or overtrump the 'Newcastle programme' produced in October 1891 by the Liberal caucus. In March 1891 he had launched the proposal for contributory old-age pensions on the German model, and the unofficial parliamentary committee set up to elaborate it came out in May 1892 with a scheme for five shillings a week at sixty-five. In the campaign itself he used his well-tried method of a series of previously prepared speeches, adding up to a programme, which could be discharged on successive days, including in this list workmen's compensation, district and parish councils, limitation of working hours and courts of arbitration. As the polling began, the Ulster Convention of 17 June in Belfast, organized preponderantly by Liberal Unionists, conveyed the evidence to all who cared to see that, if Home Rule were enacted, either the major part of Ulster must have separate treatment or it would be the signal for civil war. Chamberlain promptly raised the theme of Ulster to a central position in his warnings against Home Rule.

Immediately after the election had been fought and lost, Balfour presciently summed up Chamberlain's position for Salisbury as follows:[29]

He feels it to be absolutely necessary for his own position and for that of his party to be able to appeal to a substantive programme of social legislation.
He is ready and anxious to frame his programme on Conservative lines.
He would rather like, if he saw his way, to unite with us and sit with us under the common denomination of a national party.

Chamberlain's radical
programme brings working-
class votes to the Unionist
cause at the 1892 election

CHAPTER VIII

A Unionist

The parliament that was elected in June 1892, and the government that took office in consequence in August, were not merely in retrospect fated to failure and early extinction. They were conscious in advance of their doom to a degree which has rarely, if ever, been paralleled.

Gladstone had a majority of forty; but that was only after including the Irish Home Rulers. He would be again, and more strictly than in 1886, their prisoner. On the other side the Liberal Unionists numbered forty-seven; but they no longer, as in the parliament just dissolved, held the balance – or only on the wild hypothesis that the Liberal Party could lose the Irish but get back the Unionists in exchange. It was an unrealistic might-have-been; but it enabled Chamberlain and the Liberal Unionists to claim that Gladstone had driven the Liberal Party to sacrifice all its other historic aims to the dream of 'solving the Irish question', a dream predictably unrealizable with a majority so narrow.

When parliament resumed in 1893, Chamberlain sat no longer as heretofore on the Liberal front bench. In fact, the Liberal Unionists offered to change places with the Irish Nationalists and go over to the Conservative benches on the Opposition side. But that was too much for the Nationalists to stomach, and the Liberal Unionists remained on the Liberal side but 'below the gangway', with Chamberlain now occupying the classic strategic post at the top of the third bench.

It was from this distance that he fought his duel with Gladstone over the Home Rule Bill, of which the First Reading was moved on 13 February. At its heart lay the old unsolved because insoluble dilemma – how, given self-government, was Ireland to be represented in the House of Commons? In 1886 Gladstone had given the impossible answer 'Not at all' (p. 8). This time he preferred another of the impossible answers, and proposed that Ireland should continue to be represented in the House of

Gladstone, introducing his second Irish Home Rule Bill, directs himself to Chamberlain, now sitting in the traditional resigned minister's seat at the end of the third bench below the gangway

THE NEW MEMBER FOR
EAST WORCESTERSHIRE

VOTING AT THE BAR.

MR JOSEPH CHAMBERLAIN

MR AUSTEN CHAMBERLAIN

MR RICHARD CHAMBERLAIN.

Commons on the same ratio of members to population as Great Britain but that the Irish members should be debarred from voting on questions which concerned Great Britain only – the clause was known derisively as the 'In-and-Out' clause. An antagonist less versed than Chamberlain in all the permutations and combinations of the Home Rule conundrum would have been bound to shoot so impracticable a proposition to pieces with broadsides of ridicule.

It was in the course of the debate on the Second Reading that an incident occurred long remembered in parliamentary annals. Gladstone in winding up took occasion to congratulate Chamberlain upon the maiden speech delivered in that debate by his son Austen, returned unopposed for East Worcestershire at a by-election near the end of the last parliament. It was, the Grand Old Man said, a speech which 'must have been dear and refreshing to a father's heart'. The House observed that Chamberlain momentarily failed to conceal his emotion. Gladstone had touched a spring which opened one of the secret chambers of Chamberlain's life; for the flint-like, cold de-meanour which struck all observers was sustained by an intensely warm family life of mutual dependence and devotion. The Chamberlains were a 'clan' in the least derogatory sense of the word. Their family loyalties were total and rendered them

Austen Chamberlain (born 1863) was first elected for East Worcestershire at a by-election at the end of the 1886 parliament. His father and his uncle Richard Chamberlain (Mayor of Birmingham 1879–81 and MP for Islington West since 1885) stand at the bar ready to introduce him

Father and son in 1888

91

The famous family group at Highbury in 1906: Neville, Austen, Joe, Beatrice and Mrs Chamberlain

emotionally self-sufficient on the exterior. Into this closed world Chamberlain's third wife was wholly adopted after the years of widowerhood, across which his deep and lasting affection for his children, and above all for Austen, had helped to carry him.

By the end of June only four clauses of the Bill had been dealt with in committee, and the remainder was subjected to a guillotine which secured its passage, by a majority of thirty-four, on 2 September. On the way, however, the indefensible 'In-and-Out' clause had been dropped, leaving the position, which the advocates of the Bill in commending that clause had already declared to be indefensible, that eighty Irish members would vote upon all matters whatsoever. The effect of this *volte-face* was to expose, and not only to its opponents, the unworkability of the Bill, with the result that the House of Lords was able summarily and massively to reject it without arousing any serious public revulsion. The circumstances, therefore, in which the Lords might feel constrained to pass the Bill but attach to it the requirement of a referendum, which in February Chamberlain had proposed to Salisbury and Salisbury had favoured,[30] did not arise.

The session was preternaturally prolonged, in the hope that the Lords would massacre the government's other measures and thus enable the Home Rule issue to be merged into that of 'the Peers *versus* the People', an outcome avoided by management in which Chamberlain was deeply involved both behind and in front of the scenes. Gladstone was brought to recognise that even his last hope of carrying Home Rule – dissolution and a renewed appeal to the electorate – had no reality, and he resigned on 1 March 1894 in his eighty-sixth year. Lord Rosebery succeeded to the inheritance of a government which the Irish Nationalists no longer had any necessity to provide with a reliable majority, a Cabinet intensely divided, and a party which, in the election that must soon come, could neither fight for Home Rule nor disavow it, and was left with the unconvincing and embarrassing cry of 'ending or mending' the House of Lords.

As the prospect of the return of a Conservative government became more imminent, the ambiguity of Chamberlain's position became more unmanageable. For the third time the Conservative Party would be put under the strain, which tests all coalitions, of guaranteeing the existing seats of their allies and

The Duke of Devonshire moves the rejection of the Home Rule Bill by the Lords, 1893

93

Gladstone and Rosebery dine with the Earl and Countess of Aberdeen at Haddo House; ten years later the one succeeded the other at No. 10

allocating to them further seats still held by the enemy. After twice achieving the destruction of Home Rule and a Liberal government, it was difficult to imagine how Chamberlain could now be otherwise than a leading member of the new administration. If so, however, he must share collective responsibility for the policy of a Conservative government, and yet could not, without destroying his own moral position and alienating the ex-Liberal votes on which his party and his allies depended, disavow his essential radicalism. The problem was solved, though only just, by effectively identifying Unionism and Conservatism.

'I am', said Chamberlain at Birmingham in January 1894,[31] 'and shall be in the future, proud to call myself a Unionist, and be satisfied with that title alone, believing it is a wider and nobler title than that either of Conservative or Liberal, since it includes them both – since it includes all men who are determined to maintain an undivided Empire, and who are ready to promote the welfare and the union not of one class but of all classes of the community.' This, then, was the plan, its essence contained in the two deliberate verbal ambiguities: the ambiguity of 'Empire', meaning the United Kingdom or the British Empire, and the ambiguity of 'union', meaning political union or social solidarity.

Speaking in Birmingham Town Hall in the 1890s, watched by his wife and J. T. Bunce (died 1899), the historian of Birmingham, with hands on stick

94

After all, had not Chamberlain discovered that 'in social questions the Conservatives have always been more progressive than the Liberals'?[32] In another Birmingham speech later in 1894,* in which all his radical enthusiasms, old and new, from public management of the drink trade to universal workmen's compensation, were marshalled, he wove both utilitarianism and imperialism together into the new pattern: 'We may fairly call upon the government to use its vast resources and its great influence to secure the greatest happiness of the greatest number.' British employment, restricted more and more by foreign tariffs, would expand with the Empire. Let prosperity and power advance together, each force helping the other.

Nevertheless, the stresses mounted to a climax in the spring of 1895. Bitter attacks were made from within the Conservative Party as well as from among associates of earlier years upon this 'Unionist', who voted for Welsh disestablishment and who was once again engaged, as yet a third election appeared on the horizon, in hanging a radical programme round the Conservative neck. A furious quarrel broke out in the West Midlands over allocation of candidatures, which only the combined efforts of Salisbury and of Balfour, who led the Conservative Party in the House of Commons in close personal league with Chamberlain, were able to allay. The political crisis coincided with a collapse in Chamberlain's financial fortunes, due to the severe decline after 1890 in South American securities, followed by the disastrous investment in a sisal-growing enterprise on the Bahamian island of Andros, which his younger son, Neville, was sent out to manage.** In letters to his wife, the sincerity of which cannot be doubted, Chamberlain felt that he was on the verge of leaving public life: 'the simple fact is that the work which has sustained me during the last eight years has been, for the time at any rate, accomplished. I have largely assisted to make Home Rule impossible.'

The spell passed even more suddenly than it came. On 14 June 1895, Chamberlain was on the conference platform of the National Union of Conservative Associations in London. A week later Rosebery took the occasion of a snap defeat on an unimportant Commons question to resign, and Salisbury assumed office with Chamberlain in his Cabinet. Dissolution followed immediately, and the government was confirmed in office – for over ten years, as it turned out – by a majority of 152. The Liberal Unionists numbered 70 – not quite holding the balance. Chamberlain had completed the perilous 'middle

*Birmingham, 11 October 1894. By then Jewish immigration from eastern Europe was developing. Hence, among the rest, the early sounding of a premonitory note – that the influx of destitute aliens, lowering the working-class standard of life at home, should no longer be allowed.
** The project finally collapsed and was written off in 1896.

The former (1892–95)
Independent Labour MP for
South West Ham

passage'. With Balfour, he was the greatest power on the government side in the Commons, in the strongest administration since 1832.

The transition had been assisted – indeed, perhaps made possible – by a change in the background of the political scene, which may, if it is to be dated, have commenced with the London docks strike of 1889. It was the rise of socialism, characterized by the Marxist resolutions of the Trades Union Congress in 1893 and 1894, the Progressive Party's policies on the London County Council, and the election in 1892 of Keir Hardie as Independent Labour member for South West Ham. To Chamberlain these were 'the new Radicals', whose 'object is to merge the individual

London dockers parade in the 1889 strike

in the state, to reduce all to one dead level of uniformity, in which the inefficient, the thriftless and the idle are to be confounded and treated alike with the honest and the industrious and the capable' (Leeds, February 1894). This was straightforward Conservative stuff, and Chamberlain knew it. As he wrote to the Duke of Devonshire in November 1894,

the policy of the Gladstonian leaders has been to invite popular pressure in order that they may yield to it; and there is grave danger to anticipate that they will yield to the demands of the new [trade] unionism. . . . The Independent Labour Party are proceeding on this assumption. . . they directed their attack upon the Gladstonians and avow that they will treat them as enemies until they have accepted the socialist programme. It seems to me obvious that this will be their ultimate fate,* but in doing so they

* So, in a different form, it turned out in the 1920s and 1930s.

John Burns addresses the
striking London dockers, 1889

will risk a further secession of all that remains to them of wealth,
intelligence and moderation.[33]

It was the tide of that secession which helped to bear the Liberal
Unionists in general and Chamberlain in particular safe into the
haven of Unionism.

On the other hand, the Chamberlainite secession was at least
one of the causes which condemned the Liberal Party to eventual
extinction at the hands of Labour. A Liberal Party led by the pre-
1886 Chamberlain might have gained acceptance as a vehicle for
trade unionism and even for socialism. Certainly it could have
become the party of the working-class candidate. With the
departure of the Chamberlainites it was condemned to become
the party of Asquith.

CHAPTER IX

Colonial Secretary

When Salisbury's Cabinet was announced in June 1895 there was widespread surprise that the office allotted to Joseph Chamberlain was Secretary of State for the Colonies, albeit that office was much more prestigious then than as the generations now alive remember it. Though it was assumed, correctly, that he must have asked for it, the fact was not then known that it was the office for which he had asked Gladstone in 1886, only to be repulsed with the cutting ejaculation, 'Oh, a Secretary of State!' It was as one whose fixed determination it was to be one day in effect Minister for the British Empire (India only excepted) that Chamberlain had lived through the intervening eight years and a half, and experienced that widening of his horizons and deepening of his imperialism which made him the type and spokesman of the prevalent mood of Britain in the decades immediately before and after the end of Queen Victoria's reign.

Visiting Turkey in November 1886, he had pressed upon the Sultan a scheme of British-built railways in the Ottoman Empire to link with the Indian system, as that in turn would link with a system in China, something in which he had sought to interest colleagues in the few weeks that he remained in Gladstone's 1886 government. At the end of 1887, responding in Toronto to the toast of 'the commercial interests of the Empire', he expounded the heady theme that 'I should think our patriotism was warped and stunted indeed if it did not embrace the greater Britain beyond the seas.' He went on to touch the federal chord of the Irish debates again (see p. 78):

It may yet be that the federation of Canada may be the lamp lighting our path to the federation of the British Empire. If it is a dream – it may be only the imagination of an enthusiast – it is a grand idea ... and whether it be destined or not to perfect realisation, at least let us all cherish the sentiment it inspires.

The Colonial Secretary hands the Queen Empress' portrait to the Bechuana Chiefs at Windsor Castle. They also received a Bechuana Testament

Chamberlain's imperialism was already economic as well as constitutional. 'Is there any man in his senses', he asked the London Chamber of Commerce in May 1888, 'who believes that the crowded population of these islands *could exist for a single day* if we were to cut adrift from the great dependencies which now look to us for protection and which are the natural markets for our trade?' It is a fascinating sentence; for its reference to 'protection' and to 'markets' prefigures the use of defence and preference as means at any rate to an 'imperfect' realization of that federal

On the government front
bench as Colonial Secretary
under Balfour's leadership

dream, which Chamberlain was hardheaded enough to mistrust
in its literal interpretation.*

* Cf. his speech at Birmingham on the occasion of Lord Wolseley's campaign for conscription
(25 January 1889): 'Although I have never seen my way to any practical scheme of Imperial
federation, yet I do not deem that idea to be altogether beyond the reach of statesmanship . . .
and as the first step to any such large arrangement I am convinced that the perfection of our
means of mutual defence stands in the foreground.' An Imperial Federation League had been
organized in Britain in 1884 and Canada in 1885, and from 1889 to 1895 George Parkin
delivered throughout Australia and Britain the lectures which were summed up in his popular
work, *Imperial Federation or the Problem of National Unity* (1892).

THE FORMULA OF BRITISH CONQUEST

PEARS SOAP IS THE BEST

REG.ᴰ COPYRIGHT

The trade that followed the flag. The Pears caption read: 'Even if our invasion of the Soudan has done nothing else, it has at any rate left the Arab something to puzzle his fuzzy head over'

In the same speech to the London Chamber of Commerce he enquired, 'who is to be the dominant power in Africa?' And indeed the logic of his argument, thus stated, pointed not only to retention of Empire but to expansion. In Birmingham in January 1889 he was referring with approval to 'the constant growth and expansion of our Empire'; and he was instrumental in June of that year in the dismissal of Sir Hercules Robinson, who, as High Commissioner and Cape Governor, was resolutely opposing imperial expansion in South Africa. It was, however, Chamberlain's Egyptian visit at the end of 1889 ('Joseph in Egypt') which most evidently strengthened and stimulated his imperial thinking. In December he was writing: 'If the English occupation is maintained, I have no doubt as to the future of Egypt. . . . I hope we shall stay.' By March 1890 it had become:[34] 'We have got to stay in Egypt for an indefinite time.' In Egypt, too, he decided, with Kitchener, that the Sudan would have to be reconquered – by Britain. A free hand for Britain in Africa was

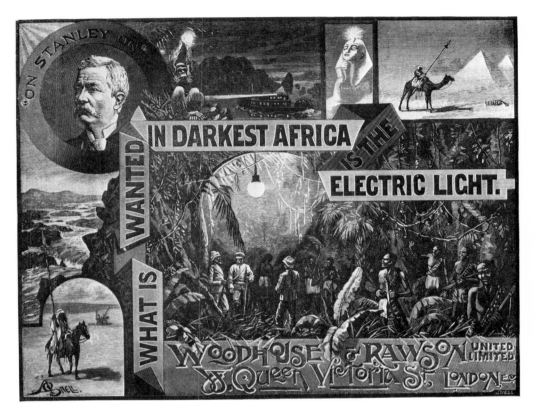

his motive in the search with Clémenceau in 1891 for – anticipatory phrase! – an *entente cordiale* with France.

Meanwhile there had occurred – in May 1890 – the curious episode of his conversation with the Canadian apostle of imperial preference, Colonel Denison, according to whose later recollection Chamberlain concluded: 'I shall study the whole question [of reciprocal preference] thoroughly for myself, and if after full consideration I come to the conclusion that this policy will be in the interests of the country and the Empire, I shall take it up and advocate it,' adding: 'Do not tell a soul that I ever said I could think of such a thing. In the present condition of opinion in England it would never do.'

The political events of the early 1890s afforded less leisure or opportunity for the further development of Chamberlain's imperial philosophy, but in his early months in office in 1895 the already familiar themes were sounded in the familiar tones. At a celebration of the completion of the Durban–Johannesburg railway in November 1895 he repeated that 'I am told on every hand that Imperial federation is a vain and empty dream', but added that 'dreams of that kind . . . have somehow or other an unaccountable way of being realized in their time'; and in the same month he called for a report from all the colonies on 'the extent to which foreign imports have displaced or are displacing similar British goods' and also on colonial 'products which . . . do not at present find a sufficient market' in the United Kingdom.

Before he could develop these ideas, South Africa swept everything else aside. In August 1895 Rhodes, Prime Minister of the Cape and Chairman of the British South Africa Company, demanded the transfer to the Company of the Bechuanaland Protectorate (p. 53), in order to enable a railway to be built through it from Mafeking to Bulawayo, which would run along the Transvaal border. Simultaneously, Kruger, the Transvaal President, having now his railway communication with Portuguese Delagoa, proceeded to penalize or prevent the entry of goods from the Cape. By November Chamberlain had agreed to grant Rhodes a Bechuanaland corridor controlled by his Company's own police, and an ultimatum from Britain had forced Kruger to 'climb down' and lift the restrictions on Cape goods. Chamberlain, however, had become convinced that an insurrection by the disenfranchised and heavily taxed British and other aliens ('Uitlanders') in Johannesburg was imminent, and he shared the prevalent belief that it would overthrow Kruger and establish a new state. On 6 December the High Commissioner, once again the now septuagenarian Sir Hercules Robinson (p. 104), was ordered by Chamberlain, as soon as the insurrection should occur, to move in and take control of events, with a view to the new state accepting British allegiance and thus opening the way to a South African federation. Chamberlain was aware that the Company's Bechuanaland corridor would, in those circumstances, afford a ready springboard for intervention in the Transvaal, and that in January two troopships would conveniently be in the vicinity of the Cape.

He did not apparently inform the Prime Minister of these arrangements until 26 December, when he sent him a letter commencing: 'I have received private information that a rising in Johannesburg is imminent and will take place in the course of the next few days,' and ending: 'if the rising is successful, it ought to turn to our advantage.' In fact he had been deep in communication, through Colonial Office officials and their unofficial contacts, with Rhodes and others in the Cape who were counting

The adjutant-general of the Egyptian army in 1890, Herbert Kitchener

on the revolt, and was aware that a force under a Dr Jameson was in readiness to dash to Johannesburg immediately the revolt should break out. Catastrophe struck when the would-be rebels in Johannesburg 'got cold feet' before Christmas and Dr Jameson nevertheless plunged into the Transvaal against Rhodes' orders on 29 December, only to be rounded up and captured on 2 January. On imperfect rumours of Jameson's intention Chamberlain wired the High Commissioner on 29 December to deter Rhodes peremptorily and on confirmation he followed this up on 31 December by an injunction of total disavowal. Significantly, he wrote that day to the Prime Minister: 'It is worth noting that I have no confidence that the force now sent, with its allies in Johannesburg, is strong enough to beat the Boers.'

Chamberlain, as references in the despatches prove, knew about everything including the Raid, except, of course, that it would take place despite the rebellion not occurring; he had kept clear only of active involvement. 'The responsibility', he minuted on 18 December to his permanent secretary, 'must rest with Rhodes and we had better abstain from even giving advice.' 'There is nothing more to be done,' he informed Salisbury on Boxing Day, when he still believed the rebellion imminent, 'than to watch the event, which we have done nothing to provoke.' The prize of a hostile republic converted into a British colony in a future federal South Africa had tempted the Colonial Secretary to the very verge of encouraging, and over the verge of condoning, armed rebellion – provided it were successful – in a state for whose external relations Britain herself asserted responsibility.

Having been unlucky, Chamberlain was immediately lucky. The telegram of congratulation which the Kaiser despatched to Kruger on 3 January raised a surge of patriotic fury not only in Britain but in Canada and Australia, to which Chamberlain responded by a bold reference to 'this league of kindred nations, this federation of Greater Britain' and which enabled him to turn the blame upon Kruger, whom the High Commissioner was instructed to warn that 'the state of things of which complaint is made cannot continue for ever' and that 'Great Britain will resist at all costs the interference of any foreign power.' It was evident, however, that there must be enquiry, all the more so because Rhodes' agents began to spread rumours of undisclosed but incriminating documents; and in July 1896, as soon as Dr Jameson's trial was over, Chamberlain moved for a Select Committee, which took evidence from February to July 1897.

Dr Jameson and Cecil Rhodes, the year before the Raid
Overleaf: the Diamond Jubilee – Queen Victoria at St Paul's

To the discredit of Harcourt and Campbell-Bannerman, who were Opposition members of the Committee, it reached the astonishing conclusion that Rhodes was guilty of 'grave breaches of duty' but that neither the Colonial Secretary nor any of his officials 'received any information which made them or should have made them aware of the plot during its development', a statement incompatible with the evidence before them, whether 'plot' referred to the rebellion in Johannesburg or to Jameson's readiness to support it. In the debate upon the report on 27 July Chamberlain actually exposed this inconsistency by going out of his way to laud and defend Rhodes as having marred transcendent services to the Empire only by 'one gigantic error'. Since Rhodes had no more authorized or expected Jameson's lone fling than had Chamberlain, there was no 'error' of Rhodes to which Chamberlain had not been privy. The passage was so incredible as to raise the question whether Rhodes had some hold upon Chamberlain after all; but by now the Diamond Jubilee had come and gone, absorbing and overshadowing everything else.

For the Colonial Secretary its significance lay in the outcome of the conference of the (then) eleven premiers of Canada and the other self-governing and still unfederated colonies. During 1896 Chamberlain had explored in speeches[35] the concept of imperial

> The **RADICALS** gave up
>
> # The Transvaal
>
> by a **Shameful Peace with Dishonour.**
>
> The **CONSERVATIVES** have **REGAINED** it for the **EMPIRE,** and wiped out
>
> ## The Radical Disgrace.

> The **RADICALS** left Egypt with disgrace; Gordon mur= dered; the Soudan ravaged by Dervishes.
>
> The **CONSERVATIVES** have **WON BACK** the Soudan; avenged **GORDON;** and put **EGYPT** in a position of
>
> ## "Unexampled Prosperity."

Zollverein, an empire of internal free trade (revenue duties apart) with protective tariffs against the rest of the world. It would imply, since the external tariffs must in principle be uniform, a common political organ or imperial council, in which Chamberlain was fain to discern the germ of federation. The Imperial Conference exploded any such notion. In common with the Colonial Conference of ten years earlier and the Ottawa Conference of 1894, the premiers made it clear that the colonies would not abandon their attachment to high protection. What they would do, however, was to offer the mother country a less steep tariff barrier than they presented to the rest of the world; and in fact Canada had already taken the initiative in April by enacting a $12\frac{1}{2}$ per cent preference for Britain with the prospect of increasing it to 25 per cent. Chamberlain seized the substitute half loaf with both hands, recording that the Conference had 'to a certain extent approved' the proposal that 'those Colonies which have a protective duty should be asked to consider whether they would not follow the example of Canada and give a preferential advantage to the mother country.' Britain for her part forthwith cleared the way by denouncing treaties with Germany and Belgium which gave those countries – and thus, via 'most favoured nation' clauses, other countries too – the right to the same terms of trade within the Empire as Britain enjoyed herself.

The Unionist record, 1895–1905, as presented by the outgoing government on election propaganda cards

113

Still, it could not escape the notice of Chamberlain that in giving Britain preference the colonies were giving something for nothing, or at any rate for nothing material. Britain could not encourage and promote their action by offering preferences in return – so long, at least, as she herself adhered to free trade.

A system of one-way preferences would have no federal implications; but political union received, especially from Canada's Liberal premier Laurier, a curious and in retrospect ominous airing. In his opening address Chamberlain had asked if it was 'feasible to create a great council of the Empire, to which the colonies would send representative plenipotentiaries – not mere delegates' and this 'might slowly grow to that federal

How the cartoonist Harry Furniss (1854–1925) saw Chamberlain's ambitions, for the Empire and for himself, at the turn of the century

council to which we must always look forward as our ultimate ideal'. 'It would be a good thing', responded Laurier, 'for the colonies to be represented on the floor of Parliament' by 'representatives allowed as full-fledged members the right to speak *and not to vote*';* but the sting was in the tail. 'This is a very great thing', he continued, 'that will have to be dealt with at no distant date if the colonies are to continue to be colonies'; for 'it will not be satisfactory to [Canada] that the present relations should continue in their present condition. Those relations must get looser or they must get stronger.' It was a dilemma which, along with the notion of reciprocal preference, the Imperial Conference of 1897 left implanted in Chamberlain's mind.

* The italics, which are mine, recall the in-and-out fiasco of the 1893 Home Rule Bill (p. 91).

CHAPTER X

South Africa

In the autumn of 1896, the earliest practicable time after the Raid and its immediate sequelae, Chamberlain intended to go out to South Africa himself and meet President Kruger in person. The personal interview, which had been attempted on the morrow of the Raid by inviting Kruger to London and which had proved abortive because of Kruger's preconditions, was to be secured by Mahomet going to the mountain. Instead, Chamberlain's destination was changed to Washington by the exigencies of a dispute with the United States over the boundaries of Venezuela and British Guiana.

Meanwhile, in breach of the Convention of 1884, the Transvaal imposed serious new restrictions upon resident aliens and took powers of arbitrary expulsion against them. Only when modest reinforcements were on their way to South Africa in May 1897 did Britain secure compliance with her demand that the offending legislation be repealed. Throughout the next two years and a half, the Transvaal rapidly increased its armaments, and the new High Commissioner, Sir Alfred Milner, arrived at the conviction that 'from a purely South African point of view, I should be inclined to work up to a crisis. . . . It means that we shall have to fight, and to fight more or less at a moment chosen by the other side, who very likely may not realize what they are doing'[36] – words written immediately after Kruger had secured a crushing re-election as president and had constituted himself virtually an autocrat. On the other hand Chamberlain, seeing South Africa in the context of the worldwide power politics of the European nations, adhered to his initial position that 'we have no reason either of right or interest which would justify a war in South Africa. . . . I do not believe there will be war . . . our business is to bring about a fair settlement.'[37]

At the beginning of 1898 Britain in her traditional unalignment was vulnerable, in the event of a major entanglement in South

One of Benjamin Stone's most brilliant parliamentary photographic portraits: the Colonial Secretary on the terrace of the Houses of Parliament

Glazebrook's portrait of Lord Milner seems to reveal the Germanic cast of his mind

Africa, both to Germany and to France, and both in Europe and in Africa. In a speech of un-ministerial candour in May 1898, long famous, from a proverbial expression which it contained, as 'the long-spoon speech', Chamberlain tried to bring this situation home to the public: 'We are liable to be confronted at any moment with a combination of great powers . . . we stand alone.' It was a situation which Salisbury as Prime Minister and Foreign Secretary and Chamberlain as Colonial Secretary succeeded during the following eighteen months in transforming into one which at least ensured freedom of action for Britain in southern Africa.

The sequence of events is impressive. In June 1898 a convention was concluded with France which ended a period of dangerous friction and overlap between the two countries in the Niger Basin. In August a treaty with Germany, the terms of which were unpublished, secured exclusive British influence in Delagoa Bay, whence the railway ran from Laurenço Marques to the Transvaal, in return for an agreement on the partitioning of the Portuguese colonial empire in the hypothetical event of its demise. A few days later the battle of Omdurman terminated Kitchener's slow-but-sure reconquest of the Sudan; but the Sudan as a whole and Britain's control of the entire Nile Valley and the Cape-to-Cairo route* were not secure until, after months of critical tension, the Anglo-French convention of March 1899 established the watershed between the Nile and Congo basins as the boundary between the French and British spheres.

The rest of 1899 was devoted to a tortuous negotiation for the purchase, by colonial concessions, of the declared neutrality of Germany in the Transvaal. The article was eventually secured at the price of Samoa, and packaged and delivered by the state visit of the Kaiser to Britain in November 1899. It was only just in time; for by then war with the South African republics had begun. It did not matter that a new treaty with Portugal, which secured its benevolent neutrality in return for a territorial guarantee of the Portuguese colonies, did not come until 1900. The mere catalogue of these events gives some impression, though partial and imperfect, of the intensity of the worldwide colonial scramble at the close of the nineteenth century, which was the environment of Chamberlain's years as Colonial Secretary.

Germany and the colonial scramble, as seen from France in 1900

* 'Young man, you will live to see the time when a railroad will be built through that country to the Great Lakes, the Transvaal and the Cape' (Chamberlain to an American reporter in New York, on the news of Kitchener's entry into Khartoum).

It would tax a Thucydides to trace the interlocking causes which during 1899 made war at last seem inevitable to Britain and the Transvaal. The pressures upon the Uitlanders undoubtedly increased during the summer 1898–99, and resulted in a direct and reasoned petition from them in March–April to the Queen, as sovereign of the great majority of them and 'suzerain' of the Transvaal. Obliged to react, the Cabinet, at Milner's own suggestion, proposed a conference between Kruger and Milner, which took place at Bloemfontein in the Orange Free State. It ended on 5 May in fiasco for which both personalities were equally responsible. Chamberlain was evidently dismayed by the break: 'You should be very patient', he wired – too late – to Milner and 'admit a good deal of haggling before you finally abandon the game.' Nevertheless he accepted the consequences and both published a lurid despatch (the 'helot' despatch) from Milner and addressed himself in his customary decisive fashion to public opinion in a speech in the Birmingham Town Hall in June, which contained the phrases, long to echo, in Birmingham memories especially, warning the Transvaal that the government 'having *put their hands to the plough* . . . will *see it through*'.

The warning appeared to work. In July a Franchise Bill was introduced into the Transvaal legislature, which, however guardedly, contained the principle of enfranchisement of the Uitlanders and their representation in the *Volksraad*. Chamberlain's relief and delight were unmistakable. 'No one would dream', he cabled Milner on 18 July, 'of fighting over two years in qualification period [for the franchise]. We ought to make the most of this and accept it as a basis for settlement.'

Why, then, when the Transvaal of its own accord had apparently gone so far, did everything turn sour, so suddenly that by 24 August Chamberlain was writing: 'It is clear that we cannot go on negotiating for ever; we must try to bring matters to a head. The next step in military preparations is so important and so costly that I hesitate to incur the expense . . . so long as there seems a fair chance of a satisfactory settlement. But I dread above all the continuing whittling away of differences until we have no *casus belli* left'? Two days after this, in another Birmingham speech in the grounds of his own house at Highbury, another memorable and more menacing phrase was used: 'The issues of peace and war are in the hands of President Kruger and his advisers. . . . Will he speak the necessary words? *The sands are running down in the glass*. The situation is too fraught with danger, it is too strained, for any indefinite postponement to be tolerated.'

The answer appears to be that British attempts to ensure the solidity of the Transvaal reforms by submitting them to a joint enquiry, with a subsequent conference between Milner and Kruger and an Anglo-Boer tribunal of arbitration, convinced Kruger that his legislation was simply to be used as an instrument for taking over the country step by step. The continuing armament of the Transvaal, the anxiety of the Uitlanders and the reinforcement, however small and tardy, of British troops in Natal and the Cape all added to the mutual misconception and antagonism. Above all, perhaps, the convictions of Milner had done their work at last. As Salisbury wrote to the Secretary of State for War, Lord Lansdowne, on 30 August 1899: 'What [Milner] has done cannot be effaced. We have to work upon a moral field prepared for us by him and his jingo supporters.' While Britain worked up by the end of September towards her own ultimatum, it was anticipated by a brusque demand from Kruger, delivered on 9 October, insisting that British troops be withdrawn from the Transvaal borders, that the recent reinforcements be removed from South Africa and that those on the high seas be diverted. Upon its rejection the two republics declared war on Britain and invaded Natal and Bechuanaland.

Upon the whole Chamberlain told truth, though less than entire truth, when he declared on 19 October to the reassembled House of Commons that 'from the first day I came into office, I hoped for peace, I strove for peace. At that time and down to the most recent period, I have believed in peace.' All the same, throughout most of the world, it was 'Chamberlain's War'.

Balfour on 17 October 1899 opens the war session of parliament

His Imperial Majesty

Like other wars, before and after, this one was to be 'over by Christmas'; but the opening weeks were weeks of disaster, militarily and for Chamberlain personally. During the Kaiser's visit, he had had conversations with the Foreign Minister, Von Bülow, as well as His Imperial Majesty, and from these he gained the impression that a *ballon d'essai* would be welcomed and reciprocated by Germany, so helping to bring Britain out of her isolation into the preferred alliance. On 30 November, the day after the Kaiser's departure, with remarkable gaucherie and innocence he accordingly informed an audience at Leicester – and throughout the world – that 'the natural alliance is between ourselves and the great German Empire' and went on to imagine Britain as linking the United States on one hand and Germany on the other in an 'understanding' which 'might do more perhaps than any combination of arms in order to preserve the peace of the world'. This imperial gaffe was greeted in Germany and elsewhere with coldness, ridicule or hostility; any less important figure in government could scarcely have survived it; and it disclosed unforgettably a provincialism and incomprehension of the continental scene, above all the German scene, which, by a historical irony, his younger son Neville was fated to exemplify on a grandiose scale.

While Chamberlain floundered in the aftermath of this indiscretion, there befell, perhaps fortunately for him, a series of military disasters in a single 'Black Week', 11–15 December, which humiliated British arms and left Kimberley, Mafeking and Ladysmith hopelessly invested. In the incredibly short space of two months this scene was transformed. Forces which amounted eventually to 180,000 men were raised and despatched to South Africa; Lord Roberts and Kitchener took over command from the discredited generals; and above all, the self-governing colonies, hitherto somewhat cool in their declared support, vied with one another in sending contingents,* an impulse which deeply impressed themselves, the mother country and Chamberlain. In triumphantly winding up for the government the inevitable censure debate on 5 February 1900, he told the House that they were 'the trustees not merely of a kingdom but of a federation. We are advancing steadily, if slowly, to the realisation of that great federation of our race which will inevitably make for peace and liberty and justice.'

He was even moved in March to address confidentially to the colonial governments an enquiry whether they considered that 'the defence of the Empire and its military and naval resources

* The final totals were Australia 16,500, Canada 8,400 and New Zealand 8,400, in addition to 30,000 raised in the Cape and Natal.

have so far become the common concern of the whole Empire . . . that joint action, or at least joint consideration, with regard to this subject should be organised on a permanent footing.' He went on to adumbrate an imperial council with salaried members 'provided by the Empire in proportion to population' who might be life peers or privy councillors. As three years before, the reaction was negative: 'the arrangement of tariff questions', replied Sir Wilfred Laurier of Canada, 'would be far more likely to bring about Imperial unity than any joint system of Imperial defence.' When, in the same month, the representatives of the Australian colonies arrived with the Bill which would federate them into a Commonwealth, the one point on which Chamberlain stuck and eventually secured a compromise was the limitation of the existing right of judicial appeal to the Privy Council. Once again, imperial unity by another route was in his mind. 'The Lord Chancellor', he told the Commons on 14 May, 'has had in mind an amalgamation of the judicial committee of the Privy Council with the appeal jurisdiction of the House of Lords with a view to creating a "Supreme Court of the Empire".'

Meanwhile, starting a bare two months after Black Week, Lord Roberts carried 'the flag to Pretoria' in an advance which culminated in the relief of Mafeking on 17 May and Ladysmith on 28 May, and the entry on 5 June into the capital of the Transvaal, whence President Kruger fled to Mozambique and thence to Holland. Before then, Chamberlain had announced, in a speech in the Birmingham Town Hall,[38] the intention 'as soon as it is safe and possible . . . to introduce these states [Orange and Transvaal] into the great circle of self-governing Colonies'. Only thus would a federated South Africa, with a federated Canada and a federated Australia, be sufficient to sustain what, in the same speech, Chamberlain called 'the unity of this great federation of sister nations that we call the British Empire'.

To carry forward the impetus, in South Africa and throughout the Empire, Chamberlain ardently desired the space of time which only a new parliament could furnish. He had his wish in the Khaki Election, declared on 17 September 1900, in which he made a dozen speeches in three weeks with day intervals between* – all in the West Midlands, except for a foray to Oldham to support, successfully, Lord Randolph Churchill's son, Winston. The new parliament gave the government the same massive base as the old had done in 1895: a majority of 134 now, compared with 129 then. Again, even more than in 1895, Chamberlain could have moved in the 'reshuffle' to any office of

* Beatrice Webb (née Potter), who formerly, before Miss Endicott's arrival, had been more than passingly interested in Chamberlain, noted (*Our Partnership*, 1948, p. 201) that 'Chamberlain had played it low, down to the man in the street, and the street has responded.'

his choice. Even more pertinently he made the almost quixotic decision to continue as Colonial Secretary.

The election had taken place in the nick of time. It was scarcely won before the war was seen not yet to be over. Defeated in regular warfare, the Boers under a group of brilliant guerilla leaders exploited their own characteristics and those of their country, together with the classic difficulties of a power which had annexed and was setting out to administer a predominantly alien population. For eighteen months it was necessary to wear down Boer resistance by a laborious process of intersecting the country with lines of blockhouses and barbed wire, destroying farms and removing the women and children to camps where initially the

'Mafeking' in Piccadilly
Circus, May 1900

mortality from disease was appalling. The worldwide, as well as
British, dismay and criticism aroused by this campaign provided
the background to the episode from which emerged the
conclusion that Britain's alignment was not to be with Germany
but with France.

Queen Victoria died quite unexpectedly in January 1901, and
Chamberlain seized the opportunity to urge upon King Edward a
new style appropriate to his vision of a 'great federation of sister
nations'. The original idea was 'King of Greater Britain beyond
the seas'; but under Canadian influence this was modified to the
form 'King of all the British Dominions beyond the Seas', which
survived until 1952. Queen Victoria's death, however, had not

The sovereigns salute the Queen's coffin at Paddington *en route* for Windsor

been so sudden that her grandson the Kaiser did not reach England before she died and join in the national grief. It so happened that immediately before this Chamberlain and the Duke of Devonshire had thrown out feelers to the German ambassador in the direction of a rapprochement with Germany. There followed an almost exact repetition of the tragi-comedy of 1899, after which the rebuffs administered by Germany and the ill-feeling engendered by the news from South Africa built up an explosive atmosphere throughout 1901. As usual the detonator was a Chamberlain speech. Rebutting foreign references to British 'cruelty' and 'barbarity', in a meeting at Edinburgh on 25 October, Chamberlain sharply turned the tables upon the critics. The storm of disproportionate protest with which his words were greeted in Germany, and which continued for months, revealed at last to public opinion the depth of the contempt as well as hatred in which Germany held Britain. Thenceforward Chamberlain was the unremitting partisan of detente with Russia and *entente cordiale* with France.

The flag they carried to Pretoria

So far as foreign opinion was concerned, Chamberlain had mined corpses, not gold, in the Rand. A French cartoon

Opposite: scenes from the South African tour – a frank greeting; with General de Wet; the Zulu chiefs at Colenso

The Boers under arms finally conceded defeat at Vereeniging on 31 May 1902, and accepted British sovereignty in return for generous financial terms to rebuild their country, full equality for the Dutch language, mild treatment of the rebellion in the Cape and Natal, and the promise of early self-government. Almost immediately Milner proposed to Chamberlain that he should visit South Africa. In October 1902 the Cabinet approved the visit, and on 25 November, with Mrs Chamberlain, he sailed from Portsmouth on the maiden voyage of the cruiser HMS *Good Hope*.

In Egypt he renewed his convictions (p. 104) of the indispensability and beneficence of undivided British rule. In East Africa he was overwhelmed by his impressions of 'undeveloped estates' as he penetrated from Mombasa into Kenya. In South Africa itself he travelled from Natal into the Transvaal and thence through the Orange River Colony to the Cape. Everywhere, in gatherings small or large, official or informal, he sought by every means to emphasize the acceptance and equality of the Boers while still insisting on the permanence of the terms of

the victory and the response and co-operation which Britons felt entitled to expect from their new fellow-subjects: 'My object is to secure in this colony the fusion of races, to make two peoples into one nation. Good citizenship should be the test of everything in South Africa.'[39] Before leaving Cape Town on 25 February 1903 he received from the leaders of the Dutch party, the *Bond*, what he described as 'assurances so full, so definite and so authoritative that I cannot doubt that their publication ... will have its effect',[40] and from the English ('Progressive') Party an unsolicited and handsome acceptance of that assurance. His parting injunction was 'to make preparation for that ultimate federation of South Africa which is destined, I hope in the near future, to establish a new nation under the British flag'.

On 14 March he landed at Southampton after four months' absence, to a triumphant welcome and a wintry political scene.

The Mansion House banquet to welcome home the Colonial Secretary and his wife, March 1903

With the South African party leaders in Cape Town

131

CHAPTER XI

Tariff Reform

In the detachment of absence Chamberlain revolved, with little satisfaction, the political events of the previous twelve months. On 24 March 1902 the government, he not dissenting however reluctant, had introduced an Education Bill in the full consciousness and expectation that it would be their death warrant. It was forced upon them by the necessity of legislation to eliminate the overlap which had arisen in secondary education between the school boards (p. 84) and the county councils – something which it was impossible to do while leaving compulsory elementary education untouched. They were thus obliged to reopen the settlement of the 1870s as between board and voluntary schools. Their decision was to unify under the county councils the whole oversight of primary and post-primary education, thus making them responsible for the standards and therefore for the maintenance – mainly out of rates – of the religious schools. The Bill, which reached the statute book, unmodified in principle, in December 1902, ran counter to the Nonconformist principles, not to say passions, on education which had brought Chamberlain into politics at the beginning. He was now on the other side. A whole section of Liberalism would be lost to Unionism.

A tariff reform meeting in the Bingley Hall, Birmingham (*cf.* p. 36). The two loaves illustrated how little a tariff would raise the cost of living. *Below:* comment on scene opposite

Almost immediately afterwards the government took another step, seen as even more suicidal electorally.* In the Budget of 14 April, the Chancellor, Hicks Beach, imposed a revenue duty (known as the shilling duty) on imported corn, in order to meet a budget deficit without unduly increasing the income and other taxes. Such a duty had a crucial history in Chamberlain's thinking. He had long held, and had told the 1894–95 Royal Commission on the Aged Poor, that 'he would finance pensions by an import duty on wheat', and that 'nothing that I have ever said or written would prevent me advocating a tax on corn for a specific purpose.'[41] Old age pensions were one of the items of his 'unfinished business' with the Conservatives (p. 86), but the corn

---

* Middleton, the Conservative chief agent, 'took a much more serious view of the corn tax than of the Education Bill' (Fraser, *Joseph Chamberlain*, p. 234).

Inspecting Coronation
contingents from the Colonies
in the Colonial Office
quadrangle

duty struck another chord: duties on food and raw materials were the precondition of any sort of imperial preference.

Four days before Chamberlain was to speak in the Birmingham Town Hall on 16 May 1902, a unanimous resolution in favour of reciprocal preference had been passed in the Canadian Parliament in anticipation of the Colonial Conference in June which would accompany Edward VII's coronation. In his speech Chamberlain referred with ridicule to Liberals who had attacked the corn tax just because it did create 'the possibility of preferential relations with our colonies'. He then took occasion to conclude, with unmistakable relevance: 'If by adherence to economic pedantry, to old shibboleths, we are to lose opportunities of closer union which are offered to us by our colonies, if we are to put aside occasions now within our grasp, if we do not take every chance in our power to keep British trade in British hands, I am certain that we shall deserve the disasters which will infallibly come upon us.'

The coronation was deferred, but the Colonial Conference was not. Chamberlain repeated his proposals (p. 115) for 'a real council of the Empire to which all questions of Imperial interest might be

referred'[42] and for imperial contributions to defence. To these the Conference returned a stony response. On the contrary it resolved, while 'recognizing that in the present circumstances of the colonies it is not practicable to adopt a general system of free trade as between the mother country and the British dominions beyond the seas', to 'urge respectfully on H.M.G. the expediency of granting in the U.K. preferential treatment to the products and manufactures of the colonies either by exemption from or reduction of duties now or hereafter to be imposed'. The prime ministers and above all Sir Wilfred Laurier left no doubt that their urging was serious.

It fell to a new government, in which Balfour had replaced Salisbury and Ritchie had replaced Hicks Beach, to resolve whether this was or was not to be the outcome of their review of the fiscal system. After a Cabinet meeting on 19 November 1902 Balfour informed the King that after 'long and elaborate discussion . . . the Cabinet finally resolved that, as at present advised, they would maintain the corn tax but that a preferential remission of it should be made in favour of the British Empire.' It was alleged later that the new Chancellor was the only

The Colonial Conference, 1902. Sir Wilfred Laurier sits on Chamberlain's right dissentient.[43] But having been defeated at the season when chancellors are weak, he renewed the battle with success when chancellors are strong – on Budget eve. About the end of February 1903, before Chamberlain was back from South Africa, Ritchie warned the Prime Minister that he would resign unless allowed to repeal the corn duty; and at Cabinets on 17 and 31 March he forced the Cabinet to resile from its decision of the previous November, with the sop to Chamberlain of reserving his right to argue for re-imposition when the matter had been further studied in the summer. Accordingly the Budget on 23 April removed the duty and with it the basis for imperial preference.

For reasons which are withdrawn from the possibility of our knowledge, Chamberlain had failed to resign, though his personal prestige stood at its height and his resignation, rendered not only intelligible but publicly justifiable by his colleagues' failure to prepare the way for imperial preference, with all the overtones of imperial unity attaching to that, would have saved him from personal humiliation. He would have been the hero – the martyr – of Empire. The consequences of his failure to resign were never to be repaired.

Thus baffled inside government, he resorted to his ancient weapon of the public speech, and that on his classic stage, the Birmingham Town Hall. As with many speeches which detonate tremendous political explosions, he said nothing in it that he had not said before, and in public. It was the occasion which was the fulminate. After taking his hearers on a review of the roads to imperial unity which were not open, he concluded with the offer of preferential duties that the colonies had unanimously made and with their expectation that in offering Britain preference they would be protected against retaliation such as Germany was already exerting against the Canadians: it was protection that Britain could only afford to the colonies if she was herself in a position to raise retaliatory tariffs against other countries. His conclusion was that Britain must choose between maintaining free trade in 'absolutely a new situation' or decide to 'recover our freedom, resume the power of negotiation and if necessary retaliation whenever our own interests or our relations between our Colonies and ourselves are threatened by other people'. 'I desire', he said, 'that a discussion on this subject should be opened' and he warned the Opposition that at a forthcoming election they would 'find that the issues which *they* propose to raise are not the issues on which *we* shall take the opinion of the country'.[44]

A typical propaganda postcard of the Tariff Reform League

The FOREIGN IMPORT SHOWER.

JOHN BULL :—"IF I STAND THIS MUCH LONGER, I SHALL GET MY DEATH BLOW."

Chamberlain dreams of the transformation when, with his tariff policy, he takes the reins of the lion and unicorn. A postcard series entitled 'Joseph the Dreamer'

The peroration contained a fatal ambiguity. The Cabinet's decision formally covered Chamberlain's advocacy of 'a discussion', which he repeated in the House itself the following week in an old age pensions debate by referring to 'that review of the fiscal system which I have indicated as necessary and desirable at an early date'.[45] But if the government were to 'take the opinion of the country', they could do so only if they themselves had come to a conclusion, and that, the conclusion which Chamberlain presumed, namely in favour of reciprocal and retaliatory tariffs, which presently became known as 'tariff reform'. Morever, unless the 'discussion' were to be conducted behind closed doors in the Cabinet room, which was absurd, it would have to be fought through in public between the proselytizers and the anti-proselytizers, who could not be prevented from forming two antithetical wings, and soon two opposing camps, in the Conservative and Unionist ranks. In a further parliamentary debate on 28 May Balfour sustained Chamberlain's right and duty to open up the question, and he and Chamberlain expressed themselves as unaware of any disagreement with what the other

said. So long as the session continued, the respective protagonists in the government contrived, not without embarrassment, to avoid direct personal conflict. In the country, however, and particularly inside the Unionist ranks, campaigns got under way on both sides, literature was prepared and research organizations created, especially in the tariff reform cause.

Once the session ended, it was clear that the conflict inside the Cabinet itself must be resolved. On the eve of its meeting on 14 September, Chamberlain wrote to the Prime Minister intimating that unless the decision were in favour of preferential as well as retaliatory tariffs, he 'must leave the government', a course which would reduce Balfour's difficulties and give Chamberlain the freedom of action he had failed to secure by resignation in March.

Accordingly, when the discussion in Cabinet showed the Prime Minister unwilling to support a preferential tariff as a matter of practical politics, Chamberlain announced that he would resign, albeit continuing thereafter to support the government as a private member. As he had done seventeen years before, Chamberlain had once again left a government to take the leadership of a cause which foreseeably would reshape the party system. On this occasion, however, a comedy of errors was enacted which involved the government in humiliating confusion and marred the opportunity that Chamberlain sought.

In anticipation of the Cabinet, four of its other members – Ritchie, the Chancellor of the Exchequer, Lord Balfour of Burleigh, Lord George Hamilton and the Duke of Devonshire – had agreed to resign collectively if the Cabinet acceded to the principle of preference. Unaware that Chamberlain was drawing the opposite conclusion, they took his demand to be the upshot of the debate, and all four sent in their resignations the following day. Balfour accepted those of the first three, and appointed Austen Chamberlain to succeed Ritchie; but he induced the Duke to withdraw his resignation, by informing him of Chamberlain's and indicating that in a forthcoming speech at the Party conference at Sheffield on 1 October he, Balfour, would 'come out against preference'. He did in fact on that occasion, while advocating fiscal reform, declare that he could not propose preference to the country 'because I believe the country will not tolerate a tax on food'. All the same, the Duke, whose conscience had been pricking him, resigned. Balfour's juggling had come to nothing, and the government and the Conservative and Unionist parties – though their rank and file appeared to be favourably disposed to tariff reform – were irretrievably split, with the Prime Minister stranded ignominiously in between.

Constituency opinion from then on became increasingly menacing to the future of government MPs and candidates who opposed tariff reform. 'It seems clear', wrote Lord Hugh Cecil, who was one of them, to the Duke of Devonshire in December 1903, 'that except in exceptional circumstances no free trade Unionist is likely to be returned to the next parliament unless by the help of the Opposition',[46] and abortive contacts actually took place between the Duke and leading Liberals. As no realignment, however, such as had occurred after 1886, took place, individuals sought their own salvation by changing parties outright; in April 1904, for example, Winston Churchill was adopted as the Liberal candidate for Manchester Central. The Duke's position at the head of the Liberal Unionist Association became untenable; and when he resigned in May 1904, his place was taken by Chamberlain himself, who set about turning the Association into a campaign engine for tariff reform.

The week after Balfour's Sheffield speech, Chamberlain delivered at Glasgow the first of a carefully calculated series of

Before his ambiguous speech at Sheffield Balfour sees Chamberlain instead of himself in the mirror, while Disraeli looks grimly down. A postcard cartoon

twelve speeches in the major cities of Great Britain. They were modulated for variety and to cover different aspects of the case at different length. In theory the campaign was conducted within the Conservative and Unionist ranks and the respective bigwigs were carefully invited; but in substance Chamberlain was appealing over the parties to the electorate:

I am quite sure that *my people, by which I mean not necessarily Liberal Unionists but my supporters in the country*, will not take any slight to me lying down, and the result of such cowardice as some of the Conservatives seem to contemplate will be certain destruction of the government and a breach which it will take years to heal.[47]

Reciprocal preference

The speeches balanced the imperial theme ('it is only by commercial union, reciprocal preference, that you can lay the foundations of the confederation of the Empire to which we all look forward as a brilliant possibility') with the preservation of Britain's export of manufactures ('they [the colonies] will reserve to us the trade which we already enjoy. They will arrange for tariffs in the future in order not to start industries in competition with those which are already in existence in the mother country') and the power of retaliation ('the protected countries which you have been told . . . were going rapidly to wrack and ruin have progressed in a much greater proportion than ours'). In order to counter the charge that tariffs would raise the cost of living Chamberlain proposed to offset them with equal reductions of the tariffs on tea and sugar, where reciprocity was not envisaged; but thereby the revenue which once (p. 132) might have financed old age pensions and other social benefits was eaten up. It was now a frank appeal, consciously designed to outbid that of socialism, to the workers: 'I trust the working classes of this country, and I have confidence that they, who are our masters electorally speaking, will have the intelligence to see that they must wake up.'[48]

The manner in which electoral opinion would be tested attracted more and more attention as 1904 wore on and the popularity of the government continued to ebb. 'I wish this country could take tomorrow', said Chamberlain at Birmingham on 12 May 1904, 'a plebiscite, a vote of the people of this country as to whether or not they would have the change in our fiscal system which I have proposed to you'; but since they could not 'affect the instrument with which we have to work', the tariff reformers must seek to make that issue overshadow all others even at a British-type general election by the precision and boldness of their programme. 'If it does not serve us well this time', he hinted ominously, 'we will keep it in reserve for the next.'

It was not to be the last occasion in British political history when a plebiscite or referendum was glimpsed as the means of averting or healing an unbridgeable party division over a major issue by referring it directly to the electorate and thus securing a verdict to which either side in the argument could defer without loss of face if defeated. For a party in office, however, the device of a referendum raises a painful dilemma: is the referendum to be held before the government act, or is the government to act subject to validation by a subsequent popular vote? No doubt it was some such reflection which led Balfour to promulgate – on 3

October 1904 at Edinburgh – a proposal as bizarre as it was disastrous. The Colonial Conference of 1902 had adjourned to 1906. Let the electorate, he proposed, be invited at the next election to give a mandate for the Colonial Conference to meet free of objections in principle, on Britain's part, to any aspects of protective or reciprocal tariffs. Then let whatever was called for by the Conference be put to the electorate at a second general election before anything was enacted by parliament.

Chamberlain affected to regard this as a deeper commitment by Balfour to the preferential principle; but logically he repudiated the necessity for two elections and for the British electorate having to wait till all the rest of the Empire had spoken. Through the closing months of 1904 and the opening weeks of 1905 he conducted a second great speaking campaign, in which two new notes were struck. One was the appeal to the farmer and the farm labourer, who now, unlike the days of Cobdenite free trade, 'has the vote, can make his voice heard, and carry elections in many counties': for them too, like the urban proletariat, protection – for that was increasingly the implication – was advantageous. 'The watchword', he concluded a speech at Welbeck on 4 August 1904, 'in the agricultural districts is this, "more profit for the farmer, more employment for the labourer, and cheaper food [because of the offsetting reductions] for his family".' The other note was heard at Limehouse in December. It linked control of immigration with protection: 'You are suffering from the unrestricted imports of cheaper goods. You are suffering from the unrestricted immigration of the people who make these goods.' He concluded: 'I have sacrificed the power and influence which office gives in order to be able to put before you this question of fiscal reform free and untrammelled by any party connection. I say that I have done my duty; it is for you to do yours. What will you do?' (A voice: 'Make you Prime Minister.' *Cheers*.)

During 1905 the increasing imminence of a general election and the consequent polarization between free traders and tariff reformers on the government side put almost intolerable pressure on the Prime Minister to declare himself – a declaration which would only favour Chamberlain's cause. Defeat through the break-up of the government supporters in face of Opposition motions on fiscal reform was only agonizingly avoided in March and again in May. On 2 June at the Albert Hall Balfour went so far as not only to commit himself to 'retaliation' but to describe 'that other great branch of fiscal reform' which 'stirs and ought to stir a responsive fibre in the heart of every citizen of the Empire' as 'the most urgent of all the great constructive problems with which we have to deal'. For a time even the possibility of Chamberlain rejoining the government before the election was seriously canvassed; but in the end Balfour found it impossible to shake off his Edinburgh commitment to a double election, with its implied neutrality or lukewarmness towards tariff reform at the first of the two elections – the only real one. After the National Union had passed a Chamberlainite resolution on 15 November at its annual conference and Chamberlain in a series of speeches had hung protectionist declarations round the Prime Minister's neck, the prospects of a further parliamentary session appeared intolerable. On 4 December 1905 Balfour resigned, and his successor, Campbell-Bannerman, formed a Liberal government and dissolved.

At the election of January 1906, the Conservatives and their Unionist allies were annihilated, returning with only 157 members; but the Unionists held all seats in Birmingham with increased majorities, and no reading of the results could be made to indicate that tariff reform had been a handicap to candidates who espoused it resolutely. In fact tariff reformers numbered the majority, 102, of the remnant that appeared on the Opposition benches.

Balfour himself was unseated, and naturally the question of his continued leadership was a live one. While Chamberlain stubbornly maintained that he would not oppose Balfour, both for the sake of long association and loyalty and also because a group which was seven-tenths Conservative must be led by a Conservative, he was, nevertheless, determined, as soon as the new parliament should meet, to have it decided by as large and representative a party assemblage as possible whether it was to be his full-blooded version of tariff reform or Balfour's equivocation that should prevail as the Opposition's policy. At the last moment Balfour capitulated and in a letter accepted 'that fiscal reform is and must remain the first constructive work of the Unionist Party; that the objects of such reform are to secure more equal terms of competition [retaliation] and closer commercial union with the Colonies [preference]; and that . . . the establishment of a moderate general tariff on manufactured goods . . . and the imposition of a small duty on foreign corn . . . should be adopted if shewn to be necessary for the attainment of the ends in view.'

Chamberlain had imposed his policy once again, more strikingly than in 1886–95, upon the Conservative Party; but this

time it was a Conservative Party in ruins. For the first fortnight, until Balfour returned as member for the City of London, Chamberlain led the Opposition, and afterwards he remained the most effective operator on its front bench, taking in particular a large part against the Education Bill (later to perish in the Lords) which sought to amend the fatal Act of 1902 (p. 132) by transferring all elementary voluntary schools to the public authorities and excluding denominational instruction in them from school hours.

Partly a series of minor illnesses and partly the aftermath of defeat prevented Chamberlain from enlarging by speeches in the country the newly agreed basis for advocacy of tariff reform; but on 7 and 9 July he celebrated his seventieth birthday and his thirtieth year as member of parliament by a banquet in the Birmingham Council House and an enormous meeting in the Bingley Hall which outstripped even Gladstone's (p. 36). His speech ranged over his political life from the start, through the struggle against Home Rule to the abandonment of free trade and the grimmer environment of the twentieth century.

Still 'We are seven'. Birmingham at the 1906 election returned Unionist candidates for all seven seats. Declaration scene in Victoria Square, with the Town Hall and Chamberlain monument behind

145

Chamberlain and his wife tour Birmingham in an open carriage on his 70th birthday

Relatively, in proportion to our competitors, we are getting behindhand, and when the tide of prosperity recedes . . . and a time of depression follows it, the working classes especially will be the sufferers, and we shall find then that it will be impossible, without a change, to find employment for the constantly increasing population of these islands. The remedy is at hand . . . we can extend our trade in the best markets, with our best friends. We can benefit them in trading with them while they give us reciprocal advantage in the preference which they give for our manufactures.

In his peroration he returned to the theme of federation.

First chancellor of the University of Birmingham (charter 1899)

By a commercial union we can pave the way for that federation which I see constantly before me as a practical object of aspiration – that federation of free nations which will enable us to prolong in ages yet to come all the glorious traditions of the British race. . . . The union of the Empire must be preceded and accompanied by a better understanding, by a closer sympathy.

Special photography at the British Museum, Victoria and Albert Museum and the Guildhall Library by J. R. Freeman & Co.

Index

Page numbers in italics indicate illustrations